RELEASE:
A Couple's Growth
Workbook

By Christa M. Hardin, M.A

RELEASE: A Couple's Growth Workbook
Copyright © 2015 by Christa M. Hardin
Printed in the United States of America
First Printing, 2015

ISBN: 1517100240
ISBN-13: 978-1517100247

Reflections Counseling Center
www.reflectionscc.com

We hope you enjoy this Reflections Counseling Center publication. Our goal is to create and promote writings that will bring health, hope, and healing to those who read them. If you have any questions or comments about this book, write to us at reflectionscounselingcenter@gmail.com

DEDICATION

This book is written for married couples all over who have vowed to spend their lives together. May this book bless you and be part of keeping you together on the journey, make you remember why you chose your mate, and help you to find your way back to or deeper an already loving union.

I dedicate this book to the honor of my late mother and my parents' marriage. Their challenges inspired me to be a marriage counselor. In the later years, I saw them succeed in reaching the ultimate Prize as dad leaned on the Lord to bring mom beautifully through the finish line.

I also dedicate this book to my husband Wes who has given me more wonderful memories than I could *ever* count as well as joined me in the amazing blessing and opportunity of being a parent to our three incredible children.

Finally, this book is dedicated to God, who through Christ gives me everything I need to live, to learn, to love, and to thrive!

CONTENTS

Preface

Thousands of newly married couples release butterflies at their weddings each year, displaying a beautiful and symbolic gesture of rebirth. Each time, something complex, fragile and magnificent has been derived from something more solitary and simple. As a romantic at heart, I love this beauty and symbolism. I am not alone either, as evidenced by its popularity. The simple act of releasing these treasured creatures into their open-sky destiny makes ladies tear up, men laugh, and children squeal with delight.

The butterfly metaphor works well not only for the newly forged path of married life together but also for those who have walked down the relationship road till it's worn-out, dusty and in need of new lift-off. Whether someone has been spending their time concentrated and alone, like the caterpillar does in their cocoon, or whether they are still learning about what it takes to be a beautiful couple together, I believe that *all* married couples are meant to have a wonderful adventure together in the big wide open.

Only with growth and safe time together learning, however, can couples really soar. Take some time with me then, to settle into a cocoon of sorts. Allow this time of learning to release the old, to forge the new, and to be a safe-holding zone while you learn some very important things about yourself, your marriage and God. After you have done this, you will blossom, and though your marriage won't look the same, the resurrected marriage that surfaces will be far more beautiful and fragrant. It will also be an important symbol of God's covenant faithfulness to His children. To see a butterfly floating by is always such a spectacle, and this is how a healthy marriage is too, a rare but treasured sight.

Reading these words, you may not even be able to imagine your marriage looking beautiful. However, every marriage can thrive again or for the very first time if you spend time and make efforts at working out your issues in a healthy format. Many couples, however, don't know where to begin. This book is a very good place to begin that journey or to pick up where you left off if you read my first marriage manual, *RELATE*.

This book, *RELEASE*, is written for the committed couple who keeps getting stuck, sometimes because they just don't know how to show love, but more often because even with the basic knowledge set of healthy relating, they still aren't doing it. Couples or individuals reading this book may already know their own and one another's favorite ways of showing love and they may already know about the importance of date nights and both healthy and unhealthy conflict styles. Yet somehow they persist in wounding themselves and one another in multiple ways.

In *RELEASE*, I show you how to stop this unhealthy cycle, to replace bad habits and tendencies with a new, healthier set of standards for the marriage relationship and to understand your own needs for soul care.

As such, this book is intended for couples and individuals who are married or strongly considering marriage. It will help you to flourish maritally even in the midst of a stressful life.

Don't wait to blossom until things are perfect for you. There were many times in my life when I wanted to blossom for the Lord, trying to wait until things were perfect in my life before doing so. Through prayer, God revealed to me that growing is for *every* season, not just the easy ones. In fact, we grow through trials, as we read in James 1:2-3,

"Consider it pure joy, my brothers and sisters, whenever you face trials of many kinds, because you know that the testing of your faith produces perseverance."

Therefore you *can* endure and even thrive during the difficult moments of life, such as when parenting unruly teenagers, when working opposite shifts, when moving, throughout hard pregnancies, job losses, illnesses, affairs, addictions and grief situations.

The time is now. God wants something better for you. He wants to bless you, for you are His special child.

I hope you will join me in releasing the old hurts that hold you back from a wonderful marital destiny. I hope you take this wonderful opportunity to move onto something bigger and better for your marriage and for your life.

READY TO RELEASE?

I like to use various nature and athletic analogies throughout this book as helpful marital metaphors. Every couple is different, just as every landscape or training event is different, and for all couples, there are some major areas which need training, pruning or weeding, even if there is already *some* growth or health there. If you do not have *any* positive areas in your marriage, before beginning this book, I recommend taking a few weeks to read my book *RELATE* for starters and then to commit to beginning the *RELEASE* journey.

HOW TO READ THIS BOOK

Throughout this book, I have used a simple acrostic to help you remember the tools it takes to release. Like the Psalmists in the Bible knew as they regularly used acrostic formatting in their verses, humans need memory aids sometimes. Even after you are well on your way to releasing well and thriving as a couple, there's a pretty good chance you will need these reminders from time to time. Please know that I have included all the points relevant to success within this memorable framework.

In *RELEASE*, you will learn to;

R – Rest Together & Apart
E – Effectively Communicate
L – Let Go of the Past
E – Enjoy Sexual Intimacy
A – Attach Well
S – Serve Christ & One Another &
E – Endure To the Finish Line

In each chapter you will see, in addition to the main sections covered, examples from couples based on real life interactions I have had from over a decade of couples work. Names have been changed and none of the book's examples are truly about any *one* person, but all situations are very real and reflective of many, many couples whom I have had the honor of working with.

Special *LOVE NOTES* from me are included in each chapter that will help you get through sticky moments along the way, as well as a plenty of words of truth from the Bible verses surrounding these topics.

Take time to process the words from Scripture and also keep your Bible handy as you read so you can look up referenced Scriptures in the text if you want to know more about what God says.

Each chapter also has plenty of journaling space, and I recommend that each spouse have a copy of this book so they can journal individually, although one copy with a notebook for each spouse is also sufficient. If you are reading electronically, you should use a computer-writing program or notebook as well. Simply writing down your goals increases the likelihood of them happening, so even if writing isn't always fun, it's certainly a practical tool for your growth!

It is helpful to take time in this book to approach chapters on a weekly basis so you don't lose momentum or forget where you were on the journey. If you complete one chapter each week, you will have completed approximately two months worth of material in all (seven weeks, plus a final segment for making sure you understand everything well). Feel free to take more time on each chapter if you like to move more slowly. If you're anything like me and you like to read ahead, feel free to do so but come back and slow down, remembering Rome wasn't built in a day, gardens can take many seasons to thrive, and growing in marriage is a wonderful and extensive journey!

I recommend reading this book together as a couple if possible and then spending time processing it with a Christian counselor or coach throughout the designated reading time period. It isn't necessary of course to work with someone, but if you do, you can expect another layer of accountability, encouragement and guidance for the journey. Minimally, share your chapter notes with one another at home each week if you plan to complete the book together so you can decide what can be intentionally incorporated.

Now that you are on your way to releasing, take a deep breath and say this prayer aloud together or on your own for God to help you in this journey!

Dear Lord,

Thank You for showing me how to grow in my marriage and with You. Please help me (us) to find any troubling causes of our marital conflict and to repair those issues with Your help. We will give You glory for the outcome, and we expect You to do wonderful things. Thank You for the opportunity to study and to learn more about ourselves and You in this time. Amen.

Chapter 1

Rest Well Together

"Come to bed, honey," Kari's husband Jason called to her one Sunday night.

"Just one more load of laundry," she called back as cheerfully as possible.

Her husband was snoring by the time she returned forty minutes later. Yawning, she looked at the clock. It was already 12:30am. So much for time together or talking about that problem they meant to address now that the kids were asleep. There *never* seemed to be any time to connect between the different work schedules, the amount of time taking children to events and serving at church, the extended family needs or even just to finish work. Kari kissed her sleeping husband and wished for more true rest together. Thankfully, on her nightstand was this book and so the journey begins.

GET YOUR BEAUTY SLEEP

In order to reduce the stress in your relationship and to allow your marriage even the *time* to thrive, you need to spend time resting, both together and apart.

First take a moment to examine how you are doing when it comes to finding time to rest individually in your sleep patterns. If you are anything like most Americans, you probably get a little under seven hours of sleep a night. With increasing technology, I suspect those hours are decreasing. However, with new sleep wristbands and apps you can attach to your phone temporarily, you can now track your REM sleep to record your rest patterns more accurately if needed. Shoot for a healthy seven to eight hours of sleep per night and if you're not even close, start with a sleep specialist and try to get some dates on the calendar for appointments that will lead you back to a healthier sleep pattern.

The reason I begin a marital manual with this point is that a lack of rest will infringe upon everything, including your physical health and your marital health if it is a serious issue. Remember, aiming for around seven to eight hours of sleep a night will help fuel you for the journey toward both sweeter dreams and reality!

When you're not asleep, the other sixteen hours of each of your days are likely spent working, grooming, eating, showering, doing errands, paying bills, doing household and yard chores, taking children to athletics, church or music lessons, doing Bible studies, carpooling to school and other tasks.

When it comes time to relax, it's easy to see why you only have a small window of time left over in which to have fun with your spouse, right?

Though many people scoff at the idea of resting together since people are so busy with these things, most of us truly need a rest time both alone and together, in addition to the eight hours of sleep. *Scoff all you want, you are better off as a couple with some down time together.*

Don't just take my word for it though. God says in the Bible that couples needs to rest together. He even rested in the Garden of Eden (Genesis 2:2), the first setting for a couple, and we hear about the need for rest before we hear about any of the other biblical stories. That's another reason why I include this essential point here first. Let's think together now about your time for resting together more deeply.

ASSESS YOUR REST

Imagine you were stuck on a desert island. Who would you want to be with and why? This is an internal exercise not to be overanalyzed as spouses. It's simply a way for you to recognize your down time and who you enjoy spending it with.

If your significant other doesn't pop into your head immediately, you probably aren't resting well together, because if you were, you'd be able to envision the two of you working hard in tandem to find an escape plan of course, but also to imagine times relaxing together on the beach and just being the best of friends. If someone else is in that mental imagery, you shouldn't worry or panic, just allow yourself permission to like your spouse again as you consider this book as a new chapter of life.

Most likely, if your spouse isn't coming up in your mind as your top favorite person, you may both be lost in the mad rush so much that you don't have any time together and you don't even feel like you know each other anymore. You may feel that you have nothing in common. All hope is not lost. It is now a perfect moment in time to refine your schedules.

Your relationship needs time. What do we call a garden that is not properly weeded and watered? Wild. Nature takes its course there, and things grow and die where they will. God is manager of these gardens and His ecosystem rules ultimately, but He has given us mastership over our gardens so we can beautify them, both in nature and in our homes.

In the way He originally created these gardens of course, everything was perfect, so largely these kinds of environments can withstand hardship. However, we when we insert human sin and pollution into this extraordinary balance of God's design, our environment changes, animals become extinct, certain species of plants are lost forever and our air quality takes a hit.

The same goes for marriage maintenance. God gave us the perfect setup, with an allowance for time together being productive, and then after long days of work, or a long day on the job, He commands rest, both daily and weekly (Exodus 20:8, Ecc 9:9). When you follow these orders, you do well. On the other hand, if you forget to take time to properly nurture your marriage or push it aside, it too will grow wild and unkempt, and I am afraid in many cases, won't recover because by the time you notice it, things have already become disastrous.

Are you doing something every day to make sure you nurture your relationship? Maybe you spend quality time (or if you read my first book, 'Relate' time) together, which is roughly ten hours of no-stress time a week, and if so, great job!

If you aren't spending quality time together, try to set this standard of ten hours per week (or another reasonable standard) together to rest and recuperate from the daily grind with your spouse. This is less than two hours a day, so it should be reasonable, even if you have to divide it up into seemingly strange segments to make it happen.

Love Note: Make sure you also set some time aside to relate with God both praying and reading His Word every day too, as this relationship between you and Him will fuel your marriage and all other relationships. The Bible says we should "Pray without ceasing" in 1st Thessalonians 5:17, which means a simple Bible study or devotional in the morning alone won't fuel you for the day's journey. Keep fellowship open with God all day so you can find refreshment, wisdom, friendship, and love for both the difficulties and treasured moment alike.

If, after trying to get proper sleep and quality time together, you still don't actually rest well, let's take a moment to think about what's happening. Maybe it's a one-sentence answer, "Because I have two jobs and four kids," or maybe it's a deeper reason, "Because I have a nagging sense of guilt for resting," or "Because growing up, when my parents rested, it always seemed so unhealthy since they were addicted," or "Someone told me I was lazy when I rested." Whatever your problem, unspoken fear or belief about rest, take time to process it here.

_____

_____

_____

_____

Let's look together at what God has to say about both individual rest and marital rest in these verses, "Come to me all you who are weary and burdened, and I will give you rest." (Matthew 11:28) and "Enjoy life with the woman whom you love all the days of your fleeting life which He has given to you under the sun; for this is your reward in life and in your toil in which you have labored under the sun." (Ecclesiastes 9:9, *NASB*) as well as "It is vain for you to rise up early, to retire late, to eat the bread of painful labors; for He gives to His beloved even in his sleep." (Psalm 127:2, *NASB*). What do you think God is saying to you here about resting well?

_____

_____

_____

_____

DARE TO DREAM

Learning to surrender to restful times in the midst of a busy life can look different for everyone, especially since everyone's need for rest is varied. Therefore, don't judge another who needs more sleep than you or who doesn't move at your pace. However as iron sharpens iron (Psalm 27:17) it is okay to remind one another to get self-care during an opportune moment when it won't come across as nagging. Ask God for His perfect timing for those kinds of conversations. Here are some tangible tips and tools for adding more rest to your marriage.

- Scheduling quality time right into your calendar or phone as a pop-up reminder or writing it in on the daily calendar, such as an hour a day and one date night per week. Most of the time, this should be together as a couple after children have gone to sleep or before they wake up, or before or after the workday rush.
- Putting your phone down and just sitting, putting it in another room, on another floor of the house, in a spouse's pocket for accountability or just turning it off for a bit while you are together and trying to converse.
- Joining the gym together to let go of the cares and stresses of the world and to get rest from mental stresses, which are just as harmful as physical stresses if not addressed. Your teamship in this time is vital because doing favorite things together will breed positive emotions toward one another.
- Doing many of your restful outings together, such as lingering through a farmer's market, taking long drives just because you want to enjoy the countryside, or sightseeing at a mall or art gallery. This is not to say that one of you cannot enjoy an outing or shopping trip alone, or that you can't go out with a friend for coffee, but it means that the main events of resting in life are spent together most of the time.
- Taking some time out to hang out with other healthy individuals of the same gender one on one from time to time. Mentor relationships are great and afford you a

moment to breathe and to think clearly about life as well as to gain inspiration and a bit of mental rest.

- Resting in bed together, even if simultaneous sleep isn't going to happen due to differing schedules, snoring, or another matter. Go to bed together and get up together whenever possible, and in the cases of differing schedules, cuddle one another before bed or upon waking even if you have to climb in during the midst of your own awake time.
- Doing a Bible study or devotional over coffee or a healthy breakfast.
- Spending Sunday evenings or another weekly time planning for the week ahead so you can hold yourselves and one another accountable for cancelling something on a wildly busy day, for balancing your spending budget and creating schedules that will help you in doing life well. Make sure you plan in your rest times together!

RESTING IN TIMES OF SICKNESS OR CHAOS

Many times, couples are learning to be more of a team in their rest during the day-to-day average seasons of life, but during a holiday rush, a busy season at work, or when one spouse falls ill, things can head south fast. Both spouses are overstimulated, overtired, and can't even do their normal jobs well. They bicker, fight, say things they later deeply regret and basically fall apart.

If however they have already foreseen there will be difficult seasons and times (and there will be), and know how to plan for them, they can continue to thrive even during these seasons. Skipping sleep, workouts, prayer time or healthy eating just won't cut it.

Instead, in times like this, you need backup for your household. Whether it is a backup babysitter, lawn care helper, house cleaner, meal helper or tutoring for a child, remember, budgeting in for these kinds of extras is wise. In fact, you will find during times of crisis that they are not extras at all, but part of the necessary balance for your life. If you have no extra money to budget this in, ask a friend to trade during your opposite busy seasons. Don't stop until you find someone, there are plenty of people who would love the very same thing and cannot afford it.

This is necessary because when both spouses are down or chaotic, no one has the strength to help one another, and if both choose to lick their own wounds instead of wanting to (or even being able to) help their spouse in their difficult days, then marital attachment injuries, or deep wounds, can occur on one or both sides, leading to sin and sadness.

Don't feel bad, then, if you need to hire a local teen or elderly sitter or ask a parent or grandparent (who loves you both) to come and help out for a couple of hours a day while you get some r and r. Your heads may still be a little fuzzy from all you are doing but you will have chores or basic childcare needs met while you both the get the much-needed rest and work times in. The angry feelings at one another for not helping you while you are down (or spending wasted time comparing notes on who is really sicker or busier) will be far less.

Love Note: *Judging a spouse won't help anything. Coming up with a solution that does not put either one of you over your personal margin threshold for handling stress is a much better choice.*

MENTAL BATTLES

Spouses engage in mentally exhausting battles all of the time if they aren't careful, and this wastes more time than standing in line at the DMV. Yet we're not nearly as protective over our emotional time, typically. God knows that we engage in mental battles and encourages us to think positively at all times, telling us to think on things that are good, lovely, and perfect (Philippians 4:8).

If you are finding that by the end of the day, you are mentally worn out, and feel upset about the marital relationship that during the day didn't seem so difficult, and/or you have a nightmare about it while your troubled brain sleeps, don't allow discouragement to take over. God addresses this very point, saying, "Weeping may stay for the night, but rejoicing comes in the morning." (Psalm 30:5b).

Instead, remind yourself gently, saying internally to yourself, "I'm overwhelmed and exhausted. Certainly there are ways to grow in this marriage. I'm not going to let being overtired or having a bad dream or rough day make me treat my spouse differently." Instead, take it to prayer upon awakening and try to think of three things your spouse has done for you this week to help combat those feelings. If the feelings still won't go away, use your communication skills to talk it out. Chances are, however, after a fresh perspective and taking every thought captive to the obedience of Christ (2nd Corinthians 10:5), you probably won't need it. Rest can heal many fights even without the aid of further conflict resolution. If you were cranky and are having a hard time offering someone forgiveness, try to forgive in your heart before the Lord right then and there ("Do not let the sun go down on your anger," (Ephesians 4:26). and then tell your spouse in the morning. If face-to-face confrontation feels too threatening, like it may start a fight all over again, try emailing or texting as well as other methods you will read more about in the next chapter.

YOUR MODEL FOR REST

Although you have your own personality, how did you see your parents or caregivers model rest for you? Was it healthy? What did you pick up and carry along with you from their habits both verbally and nonverbally? What did you close your heart to, if anything about the ways your caregivers rested in your formative years? What did you or do you hope to carry forward from your remembrances?

_____

_____

_____

_____

Who was the safest person you could rest with growing up and why? It is helpful for your partner to know that while they are your spouse and you have hopefully left your family of origin, there were some healthy aspects you enjoyed and hope to carry forward. (Ex: *Grandpa Mark, because he took me to the ball field and we didn't need to have conversation necessarily. We just enjoyed each other's company while we kept score of the game. Afterwards, we would get a hotdog and soda and find time to talk about life at home.*). Write down the person or people here.

_____ (Person's name)

because_____

_____ (Person's name)

because_____

What aspect of this or these relationships could be carried forward into your relationship with your spouse today?

_____

_____

_____

_____

THE BEST OF THE REST

Regarding your marriage, take a moment to remember the times in your relationship when you were the most elated. How much time were you spending together? If you didn't have much time together, was it focused when you did?

Many people don't realize this but when you initially begin dating your future spouse, one of the things you start to do better is to rest well, and not necessarily physically, but mentally. You know this other person is kind, fun, and fuels you for a better living, and you realize that after the work and errands are through, you almost need to be with this person. Prior to this point many times, you are frazzled, lonely or just feel emptiness while you wait for marriage. You begin to rest and to thrive when you come together with another person who suits you, whom you can trust, and whom you can really enjoy. Can you relate to this? What did you do early on in the relationship to rest?

When you think of the time you spend with your spouse, what words come to mind as you think about resting better with them? If possible, free-associate (jot down whatever thoughts come to mind) some both positive and negative terms here (ex: rejuvenating, wearisome, worries, hopeful, complaining, schedules, disagreements, yelling).

_____

_____

_____

_____

Love Note: *Don't place a judgment on a spouse who free-associates in ways you don't understand or agree with. If there were no negative words associated with your relationship currently, there would be nothing to release so you need to let* *them process in their own way. Each person has a right to their own thought life and as we move along together, you will find things begin to shift as you work hard together to release the buildup as well as to respect their individual personhood more.*

Make a simple plan to carry something from your earliest days of health and rest together as a couple and the healthy ideas from your own childhood into this current relationship. How will you tangibly do this?

_____

_____

_____

_____

RELEASE THE STRESS

As you move along in this book, if you find that you are either cranky almost all of the time, complaining too much or "doing, doing, doing" all of the steps in this book and still not finding satisfaction, stop reading and come back to this chapter, trying to examine whether you are getting enough rest both emotionally and physically.

If you don't exercise a lot but you spend time worrying incessantly, you may actually need to increase physical output in order to rest well, since you need the mental liftoff. If you get plenty of exertion and lead a busy lifestyle, physical sleep and stopping for deep breathing and Christian meditation or reading are a wonderful way for you to find rest for your soul. In this case, make sure you work out earlier in the day to give your body time to settle down later.

Now that you are beginning a fresh new chapter of life in hopes of bringing more marital satisfaction, write down what you can do to change your current pattern of rest.

_____

_____

_____

_____

Love Note:
You can't release anything if you can't rest well.

If you need to, write your rest times into your calendar or daily to-do list. You are more likely to do it if you write it right into your schedule and then look at your schedule daily so you can see it again. If you don't have much time together because of logistics, email or text the calendar and plans to one another, spend fifteen minutes of time together having a cup of coffee or giving massages a day. No stressful topics should be broached during such rare and precious rest times. Nothing should stop you from this time.

Jason and Kari both sensed that their marriage was in major overload by the time they came to me for help. This was after many more nights and days like the one at the beginning of this chapter. As we assessed their rest, they began to list out their extracurricular activities and commitments during and after the workday and it was overwhelming even to listen to their wildly busy schedules much less for them to continue at that pace.

They were both caring individuals and perfectionists at the core so their rest time was currently only slivered, their lives were on overload and they were exhausted both mentally and physically. After they went through this chapter on rest point-by-point, and really stopped to analyze their patterns, they made slow but sure changes.

Kari worked outside the home, so the special day she took to volunteer in her children's classrooms was a non-negotiable in her eyes, as was her ministry toward her grandmother in the nursing home. Kari decided these would be her ministries, and she stopped teaching in Sunday school so she could sit through the service with her husband and stopped meal delivery to new mothers, trusting those ministries to God and others in the community.

Kari also needed more rest, having learned that her family of origin had looked down upon it, and encouraged guilty feelings for taking it. After both seeing this clearly, and prayerfully considering what God said about the Sabbath, she decided that one day over the weekend would be more laid back and instead of finishing up chores, she would still start the day with a to-do list, which in perfectionism is second nature and hard to let go of, but it would be a relationship to-do list in terms of how she could serve her family and get rest herself. She made a big family meal that day for either for breakfast, lunch or dinner and decided the other meals would be leftovers.

She and Jason decided they would protect this day and keep it for church and family building time. They played games, looked at photo albums, took walks or bike rides and just relaxed, something contrary to their natures.

Creating marital rest time spent together involved Kari making the decision to drop out of her women's book club which demanded nightly readings that were at times intensive, trading it for a monthly night out with a group of women or one girlfriend. She and Jason decided to go to bed together approximately four nights a week, settling down every Sunday night together to schedule those out. The other three nights she could catch up on chores, gab on social media, read for pleasure, or enjoy the quiet.

She decided she missed spending nightly fun time with her husband from the early days of the relationship and they decided to watch a favorite show together once per week, and to play games, go to bed early, or have sexual intimacy the other nights. Kari decided to cut her workout in half twice a week so she could recover from the sheer exhaustion of doing everything perfectly.

Jason went to work early and typically went to the gym before as well, while Kari tried to get ready for work. They didn't have a morning check in at all, so they decided they would wake up just ten minutes earlier each day and have a restful cup of coffee or tea before heading out to their different appointments. They would read their favorite devotional (www.thelife.com is a good one) and pray during this time, also catching up on anything important if necessary. Most times, however, Jason and Kari found that they enjoyed just being in the quiet time together for a moment, pausing to pray before the day's more frantic pace began. Jason even began working out from home more frequently to cut back on gym time.

Jason and Kari also realized that the children's evening activities were too time-consuming and decided that anything that could not be accomplished before dinner should be limited to one activity per week per child, so the family was able to switch piano lessons to after school and decided that next semester their son would not play travelling baseball but just do a once-a-week practice as well as games on Saturdays.

Kari's date night idea went on the calendar as a monthly non-negotiable with the idea of getting a better list of sitters so Kari's mother and father would not have to increase their giving of time. With the reduced activity, they also gained over forty dollars a month for into their budget for emergency childcare or house help from a local pre-teen sitter who could come over for a few hours if there was an extra busy time.

This was a great beginning for Jason and Kari and though your situation will look different from theirs, the marked improvements will be the same specific types of trimmings and intentional drawing back in most cases.

If you feel guilty, remember this is biblical. Jesus tells us to prune our lives (John 15:2). If we are not bearing fruit in our marriages and families, our other ministries don't matter at all. Without love toward the ones God has called us toward first, our Lord, our spouses and our children, we aren't truly living well.

But be ready, you are going to have to say no to a lot of great events and opportunities in order to prioritize your life. Do it anyway. You and your family are worth it. Let's prepare you for an even more peaceful time as husband and wife as you learn next to communicate more effectively.

Chapter 2

Effectively Communicate

"Daddy's home!" Little footprints screeched to a halt at the landing of the Thatcher home.

Lexi smiled wearily, looking up from the dishes she was rinsing. Dressed in stained yoga pants and a sloppy tank top, Lexi's hair was unbrushed and her makeup was crusted over from the night before. "Hey Pete," she said half-heartedly to her starched-shirt husband with a heavy briefcase. "Did you pick up the dry cleaning?"

Peter spent extra time hugging his eager children before he responded. "Hey hon," he said, walking up to her without making eye contact, "I forgot," he said coolly. He looked at his cell phone briefly next while taking off his shoes, "Hold on kids, daddy's trying to get his shoes off."

Lexi's voice was grating, "I told you to pick that up, Pete, how could you forget? Now I have to go out and do that in the middle of the day tomorrow."

"I think you can handle that," he said, looking around at the tornado before them both, toys strewn everywhere, an unkempt house and kitchen, and kids tugging at his legs.

"Yeah, just one more thing," Lexi said glumly. "I'm in over my ears and that would be just *one more* awesome task I can add, right before scrubbing the pots and having your parents over for dinner."

"Daddy, will you play with us?" asked an adorable chubby child with curls.

"Yes, I will," Peter responded with a lift in his voice. "C'mon guys, let's play cops and robbers."

"Ok, dinner will be ready in a few, I made your favorite," said Lexi with a half-smile, trying to be a little more positive as she remembered her husband's relationship with the children.

"Thanks," Peter said with no emotion in his voice and a small sigh.

The Thatchers may sound either familiar or extreme to you, but I can assure you, this kind of day is common to countless spouses out there, and your own ugliest marriage moments probably don't look much better.

Specifically, can you see what Peter and Lexi can't see about their communication? I bet you can find more than a few areas where they could make changes in their styles of communicating.

_____

_____

_____

_____

It's far easier to see exactly how other people can fix their problems than to see the ones in your own life sometimes, isn't it?

Since we have isolated this couple and see them as though they were in a vacuum or microcosm of existence where there are no other outside rules and judgments, we can help them more easily. As you begin to share your journey with a coach or counselor, it also helps to have that person looking inward, as they too can find some fairly easy solutions to things you may not even realize are causing deeper problems in your marriage.

I know in your life, even if you have times like the one above, there are very good reasons for the unhealthy communication patterns that have evolved. If you are anything like Peter, maybe you are tired when you come home and not only from work, but tired of seeing what you think are half-hearted attempts at family harmony from your spouse and are looking for a lift from outside society or your kids to replace the affirmations or rewards you are left without from your spouse.

If you are like Lexi, maybe you feel the whole world of family needs weighs on you and you are about to burst at the seams. Maybe your only way of getting sleep or a moment to yourself is to skip out on self-care and cleaning. Wherever you are at today, it's time to move you to a better place.

In this chapter and the rest of the book, I will weave in many tools for healthier ways of engaging so you can avoid even the unspoken collisions occurring in your home. Despite the hardships around you and the challenging internal voice telling you to give up, choosing to love your spouse and yourself will make an enormous difference in the process.

A DEEPER DIG

Communicating, or lack thereof, is very frustrating at times. Digging deeper into the garden of your marriage includes tackling communication issues, even the thorny ones. God only knows how wonderful it feels, however, when conversations offer spouses a window into one another's souls. Communication can be simply invigorating when it happens well.

However, when spouses intentionally hurt one another, the poison of negative communication also goes down deep into the crevices of those very souls. I know you don't want to be like poison to your spouse because you love them so much, and ideally, even more than you love yourself.

Despite the way they choose to behave, then, make a decision to produce good fruit in your conversation toward them. If you are being abused however, please talk more in depth about this as you process with your therapist or coach, or if you're not working with anyone, get help. Don't allow it to continue.

RELEASE THE FAIRYTALE

Words are powerful and as the Bible says, they have the power of both life and death (Proverbs 18:21). However, it's still important to release hopes for one hundred percent perfect communication at any point of a relationship between two human beings. Although Cinderella and her prince lived happily ever after, we have no reason to believe that they had perfect communication, and if you have seen any of the Disney sequels (or *Into the Woods*), you know that even royalty get in their share of tiffs in the later days.

In essence, every couple can use better communication and no one, save God, loves perfectly all of the time. Do you think you are a perfect communicator? What are your best skills when it comes to communication?

_____

_____

_____

_____

RELEASE THE NEGATIVITY

You may think you are a positive person in general, and may actually be very positive with some of the people you regularly interact with, such as your best friend or mother. This is an irrelevant point. We are trying to help your *marriage*, so marriage positivity is the relationship positivity we need to see, the others simply won't be involved in this focus.

In your marriage this week, try this exercise. <u>Say nothing negative all day every day for one week. This includes avoiding all non-verbal sighs, rolling of the eyes and tone.</u> If you can't do that for a week, try for one or two days. In this time, don't complain about the weather, his or her attitude, the stomachache you have, make fun of your spouse even in sarcasm, talk badly about their family, insult their schedule, their job, and don't say any other negative remarks either.

Instead, show love and grace. Don't being a robot, agreeing with everything in a fake manner. In fact, don't spend any time whatsoever on a negative attitude.

I would be shocked if you said that you did this perfectly for an entire week, first of all, but secondly, if you do your best, and try to keep it up for a week *sincerely*<u>, I would be shocked if it did not bring lasting changes</u>. The releasing of negativity always helps, even if it's starting to break chains below the surface. In other words, don't grow discouraged if your lack of negativity doesn't impress your spouse outwardly. Check in with them at the end of the week to see not only if they noticed, but also if it made them feel lighter or more trusting with you. You may not have correlated some of their positive behaviors toward you that were indeed a direct result of your hard work! Keep it up; don't give it to negativity for it hurts you. Make it a regular practice.

RECOGNIZE STYLES OF COMMUNICATING

Styles of communication are a leading factor of couples conflict also. Most of us began getting used to a particular style of communicating when we were very young children. The core parts of our personality develop in the first few years of life typically.

Though some of us changed in our personalities vastly since then and have (hopefully!) matured, our temperaments were likely formed to large degree.

Though this may sound ominous, God can change anything and anyone, and often does do a radical healing in individuals' lives even when there has been neglect or abuse in these formative years. However painful it is to think about it, it's worthwhile to examine how you grew up and learned to communicate, both in what you were taught and in what you were shown.

> ***Love Note:*** *It's always good to look backwards to see how difficulties influenced you, except possibly in the case of an addiction. If you are suffering from a true addiction, most clinicians believe that treating your addiction first works better than approaching traumatic family of origin issues, since bringing up a stressful past does little to curb the use of the subject of addictive dependency. Instead, try coping mechanisms that are healthier first, along with inpatient or outpatient detox, support groups for the addiction, and private addiction therapy or a sponsor. Then you will find talking about family of origin issues actually makes your load lighter versus being overwhelming.*
>
> *Take your time to do the work first, versus having to go backwards later. Shed that extra addictive weight that is holding you back from a better life!*

Take a few moments to process styles of communication in your own family of origin. How did your family communicate their joys? Family emotions could have ranged from loud whoops, celebrating with feasts or desserts, affirming one another with words, quiet, peaceful and blissful rituals, hugs, going to special places, happy tears, or gifts. When a joyful moment occurred in someone else's life, where the family structure was not as healthy, even beautiful moments were completely lost in the hurry, neglect or abuse. Either way, share here some of the best ways you can remember celebrating victories in your life or in someone else's life here. Share this with your counselor or coach.

What are some of the positive celebrations of joy you would like to carry forward into your own style of communicating?

_____

_____

_____

_____

What are some of the styles you would like to release that were overwhelming or missed the mark in another way?

_____

_____

_____

_____

Now, try to remember some of the ways your family engaged in how they shared their frustrations and stresses. This includes an even wider range of emotions, in that families can act wildly unpredictable when bad things happen to them. People argue, use abusive language, threaten, cheat, drink, do drugs, shout, neglect, withdraw, leave, become workaholics, become too close with their children (enmeshed) and/or thankfully, some positive things too, like tell their families how much they mean to them, rise up to the occasion, meet challenges head on, pray, work hard to provide, and enlist outside support to help the family through crisis. Here is some space to write down ways your family of origin communicated their pain, verbally and nonverbally (through tone or actions, not necessarily words) during stressful times.

What would you like to carry forward from your family of origin in the ways of dealing with stress? What are some things you'd like to leave behind in this arena? How will you do this? Ideas will follow in this chapter, but maybe you have some of your own or have already done things differently to large degree.

_____

_____

_____

_____

FAMILY DREAMS

If your parents or caregivers had dreams for your family, did any of those dreams coincide with the ones in your heart? What were those dreams? Ask God if any are to be retrieved in any way.

_____

_____

_____

_____

Do you have dreams for your family? Some individuals and couples have dreams they have never shared, or haven't shared in a long time. Take a few moments to talk about your communication dreams for your family. (ex: I hope we will often tell jokes around the dinner table, or I want to pray together, or I want to have Friday night bonfires, I hope for a weekly date night, I enjoy having time every day to debrief together via email or right after work, I like having no-stress relate time, etc.)

Love Note: *As you write, dream big and use present-tense language versus past tense as though these dreams and hopes are completely and forever lost to you. What is your marital mission statement? Do this with your spouse, too!*

_____

_____

_____

_____

What are some mutual ways you would enjoy being more intentional about communicating as a couple and/or family? How about ways you can bring some of the dreams to life, little by little? Take a few minutes to talk this out with your spouse and/or therapist if your spouse is unwilling.

_____

_____

_____

_____

RELEASE OLD FAMILY DRAMA

Sometimes a spouse will want to specifically avoid something in his or her spouse's family of origin, in terms of how they behaved or they may ask their partner to avoid carrying forward a habit they dislike from the family. While sometimes this is unreasonable and/or controlling to request someone make changes from their family of origin, this is oftentimes a legitimate request and should be considered as something that will not only bring health to the relationship, but to the individual who now has a chance to be primarily part of a much healthier system and to break out of the legacy ties with the unhealthy family of origin.

Write down some things you would like to let go of from your spouse's family of origin, and not carry forward into your own marriage or family. (Ex: *The parents discussed all of their marital problems with the kids and I don't want to do that*, or *The dad was nice but was gone all day long on Sundays and that wasn't fair for you*, or *Your mom bottled everything up and was depressed. I want us to talk about things*). If your spouse wants to carry it forward, prayer and compromise may be in order, so long as it is not a moral issue. If it is, talk it out with your counselor or coach if you can't come to a resolution.

_____

_____

_____

_____

NO THANK YOU!

Next, onto some specific communication no-no's! Here are some ways couples poorly communicate. Do any of these look familiar to you? Take a moment to check this list out with honesty. Be willing to walk away from the negative styles that don't help you or your spouse and from this point forward, take steps toward a healthier you and marriage!

THE WORST OF TIMES

What are some of your more unhealthy styles of communication? (Check the box next to the unhealthy styles of communication you have practiced in the past six months). Don't check boxes for your partner here, just yourself. Ask them to do the same for themselves if you are sharing a book, or ask your coach or counselor to go through the list with you.

____ Ignoring each other while speaking.

____ Staring at phone while your spouse is talking.

____ Not spending time thoughtfully processing what your mate says.

____ You avoid eye contact frequently.

____ You make large financial decisions without consulting your spouse or without their blessing.

____ You make vacations plans without consulting your spouse (for yourself or the whole family).

____ Your tone suggests you are bored.

____ You rarely, if ever, laugh while talking.

____ You don't say anything at all and let the anger and sadness brew inside.

____ You turn to another person or addiction for love and affection.

____ You have language barriers that aren't remedied (such as a bilingual marriage where spouses have stopped trying to understand one another).

____ You say, "Nothing will ever change," because you have noticed long-term negative themes and patterns in your marriage.

____ You are rudely sarcastic about your spouse's friends, family or coworkers.

____ You yell, call names and otherwise insult one another's character when you disagree about things.

What are some of your better styles of communication? Check both things you intend to try as well as positive things you already have in place.

THE BEST OF TIMES

____ Waiting until the other is finished speaking before you begin.

____ Smiling or laughing while your mate tells you a pleasant story.

____ Asking for clarification before jumping to conclusions.

____ Mirroring back what you have heard.

____ Showing enthusiasm for your spouse's conversation topics.

____ Using "I language" in conflict.

____ Taking a time-out instead of yelling or abusing.

____ Taking deep breaths.

____ Praying for one another and your marriage quietly or aloud during or immediately following conflict.

____ Offering an apology without compromising your integrity or dignity as a human being.

___Seeing a counselor or coach to help you when you get stuck.

___Asking your spouse about their day and listening instead of interrupting (female tendency - though both can) or fixing (male tendency - though both can).

___Telling your mate when you are upset but sandwiching that between highlights/good things about them.

___Talking out a conflict and compromising.

___Talking about financial goals together and holding one another accountable in large purchases.

___Planning vacations out with financial peace and nuclear family harmony in mind as opposed to planning for extended family needs first.

___Streamlining your ministry so you aren't giving out way too much or too frazzled in your giving.

___Talking out a conflict and giving your spouse the benefit of the doubt by choosing their idea over your own sometimes.

___Saying "I'm sorry" when you have offended your spouse even if you didn't intend to offend.

___Giving space when asked.

___Encouraging.

___Letting up control over a situation where your spouse is an adult who can make this decision for themselves, since it is minimal.

___Not trying to solve all of your spouse's problems for them the minute they tell you about something.

___Putting the phone down during conversation with them.

___Emailing or texting if needed to keep conflict at bay and to give some boundaries to lengthy battles.

___Journaling or calling a trusted mentor who shares your values.

___Grabbing shoes and running or exercising to release stress.

___Taking a hot bath to soften your emotional intensity.

___Offering your spouse a warm hug every day (Adding a kiss would be marvelous!).

___Putting down the heavy burdens you carry to just relax and in order to have some lighter talks.

Love Note: *Even if you have a very sarcastic way of relating to one another after reading your spouse's hopes and interpretations, don't judge one another's intent for change as "next to impossible" or laugh if your spouse checked that they do or want to do something you are doubtful about. People rarely* *change without support but on the other hand, your support can mean a lot in the way of change, so use your communication to bless them, even if at times that means simply holding your tongue!*

WRITE IT DOWN

Writing down your intent for better communication can make a big difference, so use this space to write down a couple of things you will try to do differently here, things you checked off above or other things you want to try. Revisit this list if you fail, as failures are part of life and teach us more about ourselves. Failures push us forward to growth if we just get back up again and keep trying.

_____

_____

_____

_____

HORMONES AND TIMING

Another factor that can influence communication is hormones. It's not exactly a comfortable topic but the topic of releasing stress through improving communication would not be complete without addressing the issues of hormones.

Although women don't like to be chided for acting emotional when they have a menstrual cycle, it's a worthy conversation for many couples. After all, the hormone progesterone stops and the estrogen level sharply decreases just before menstruation (www.merckmanuals.com). To expect for her to remain the same as she was before during this bodily shift may be even stranger. Track your/her cycles, and remember that when you/she brings up issues during this time, there may be more sensitivity around them and she may have darker emotional lenses on as she views the relationship. In the following week however, she will typically recover and the week following this cycle is often her brightest of the whole month, where she is more fun and vibrant, full of life and ready to win as a team again. Try to remember the good times will follow the hard days, and keep open communication about needs during this time.

A wife may say, "I need a lower back rub or loving touch during this time, since I feel emotionally bankrupt." Whatever she says or does not say this week, a husband is wise to check in with her needs and to affirm love throughout versus steering entirely clear.

In the same conversation, a husband may say, "I need you to visit your doctor to get something adjusted or for you to try to adjust your temper, since you say horrible things and make threats to break up during this time."

This is also a valid point if her temper is extreme. Just because you are different at this time, ladies, boundaries need to happen so true growth that takes this week into account can occur.

It is also a worthy topic of conversation for a husband to talk about his levels of his main hormone, testosterone in this time. Someone with an imbalance in this region may also have mood shifts or difficulties.

How do hormones (male or female?) affect your relationship? (It's okay if you differ in opinion here. Relax if this is the case, for the next question is far more important).

_____
_____
_____
_____

What can you personally work on to make sure your spouse isn't blamed for your body changes?

_____
_____
_____
_____

TENNIS IN MARRIAGE - LOVE ALL

In tennis, there is a term called "topspin" which means you put a twist on your hit so the ball will drop past your opponent so fast they won't have time to react properly. This is a wonderful tip to keep in your back pocket during a competitive tennis game. Not so much in marital strife, however!

If you aim to "win" a particular fight, by playing with the upper edge in your wise speech or knowledge like you are playing with topspin, you miss the point. Remember, you are on the same team! Similarly, when you have balls (metaphor here!) that are coming in from other courts (other people, not part of the marriage), it unfairly leaves your team member unable to return the ball (communication) property. If your spouse serves you an unfair ball because of this, do what we do in tennis and call it "Out" loudly and clearly. Then let it go by, as there is no need to return a vicious service.

If one (or several) of your parents or siblings tries to be part of your marital tennis game, don't allow it. In other words, don't even return the serve. For example, if one of your parents or siblings asks you to go on a weekend getaway with them for shopping or golfing or for some other reason, you may naturally be excited about the idea and initially share that excitement with them. Then, after you talk about it with your spouse, they aren't thrilled.

Your spouse may want to know how you are going to account for the lost time or paycheck. They may feel you already place yourself first a lot or maybe they are simply burned out. Maybe they know you have the extra money but are thinking of prior commitments or the lack of time the two of you already have.

This kind of issue happens frequently with couples, and when one of them tells their extended family member that their spouse is hesitant to accommodate for the event, the extended family member often unwittingly tries to pit their blood relative against the spouse, "I can't believe you let them control you like this. I would never have allowed this with your dad (or your mom, etc)," or "You're getting yourself into trouble. Remember when they did this (or that)? Whether it's about a trip, a job promotion, a major shift in where you will live or a weeknight commitment to something big, leave your parents and siblings out of it.

How can you do this tangibly? I certainly know family has a way of getting into your boundaries and making things more difficult to set up, so here's a simple reminder and rule of thumb. <u>Don't return the serve.</u>

When they bring any kind of a nonverbal or verbal remark up about your spouse that is negative, or comment on your own perceived marital weakness, let it go, and don't return it for anything. It is a "dead ball" and will not go over well ultimately.

Why is this? Well, first of all because it's impossible to be healthy in your marriage and to please someone who doesn't have your marital best interest at heart. By being a team player with your own spouse (except in the case of abuse), you are doing something great, something everyone should applaud. Don't expect dysfunctional and desperate extended family members or friends to get this however. You have to make this decision for your own family.

If an extended family member asks you to go on a trip or do something that is a commitment with them that will take you from your family for any amount of time and you want to go, say something to the effect of, "That sounds fun. I'll see what's on our family calendar and budget for that weekend."

Next, talk to your spouse about this event or possibility and don't place demands. Let them see your heart for your family and your desires and pray that God would help you together to make the right choice.

You may decide together that it's a really great idea for you to do something with the extended family member or friend, and because your spouse feels like you and they are a team, they may even applaud your self-care. Doing things this way is a win-win and they are happy for you.

If you just trample your own family boundaries and joint decision-making process by making plans with extended family first, you are setting yourself up for a fault. Your own.

Just remember, when someone from outside the marriage dynamic comes in with controlling attitudes, a quip, a dig, gossip or slander about you or your spouse, don't engage the serve! Talk things out together with your spouse and then consult your family member together if necessary. It is not worth your time or your marriage to do it any other way!

Love Note: *If you are discussing a touchy issue regarding extended family, it is advisable to do so in front of a counselor or coach. Who of the great players in any sport would be able to say they played their best game without their coaches' influence? Do let a coach or counselor influence you. Include God in the process as well as His word, which is the best coaching manual available to you. The others, who may be well-meaning friends and family, are standing on another court, supposed to be paying attention to their own games, or even wishing they had a game to play.*

CONSTRUCTIVE CRITICISM - THE SANDWICH METHOD

Although you know to refrain from talking negatively, and you are learning some techniques about communication styles to release and to pick up, you may be wondering *when and how* you can bring up your issues. I know you have things that bother you about one another.

There is no one perfect technique that works on everyone since people are never an exact science, and while this is precisely what makes me want to creatively study them, it shouldn't discourage you.

This is because trends in conflict management can still lead us to realize that sandwiching any issues or complaint comments between two positives compliments can really help your message to get sent appropriately and with increasing likelihood for positive change.

Another way of saying this is to "Compliment, Comment, and Compliment." In all circumstances, use this sandwich method to influence your spouse (or anyone you are trying to positively influence) and you will find your success outcomes are much better.

When you use this sandwiching method, your partner can more easily handle the blow of your felt rejection of a part of them, which often otherwise draws out fear and defense. This is probably also why the Bible says perfect love casts out fear (1 John 4:18). Jesus knows our frailty, but when we are sure of love, we no longer live in fear of another person leaving or not loving us. We in fact, also want to grow into our best self, which is exciting and so much more possible when we feel the safety net of someone else's appreciation of us even as they make a request for change.

Another great way to do the sandwich method, especially for a nervous spouse who feels they can't keep their cool or may be controlled by a more verbally powerful (or loud) spouse who can get to the boiling point quickly or upset the children, is to write a well thought out email or letter by hand. In these cases, it's important that the letters are loving and mature, showing both respect for the other in their personhood and also your own. Once something is in print, it has the potential to get into the hands of extended family members, lawyers, courts and in front of children's eyes.

In this method and all methods then, remember to both show love to your spouse and not to let your anger get the best of you. Begin your letter with a sentiment of love. If there is urgency in the matter, make a request that they read it within a reasonable amount of time (today, or "this morning" or before bed) and give them a reasonable duty to respond, "Please let me know before tomorrow morning what you think" but don't push and insist they respond to a big issue over a quick breakfast or within a crazily scheduled day.

Instead, write the letter using both your heart and your mind, asking he or she to consider your interest in the matter, and explaining your points clearly and sincerely (Don't overdo - letters should be under one page in length for the respectful effect/response you are looking for. Someone will likely be majorly on the defensive if there a list longer than one page typed out to them because it leads to a pervasive sense of hopelessness and defeat before even opening it, "She (or he) will never be happy with me so why bother even trying."

Instead, include important points, things you must have in order to maintain family respect and harmony, include things you are willing to concede or compromise on, which is part of love after all (love others as you love yourself), and finish it up with another sentiment of love.

TAKE PAUSE

If you or your spouse are too sensitive for any usage of even the sandwich method, I have two directives, one for the spouse who would like to use this method to safely communicate request for change, and one for the spouse who feels they can't handle this.

For the spouse requesting change: If your spouse asks you not to request any change right now, and seems in complete despair when you do, they are not in a great place emotionally with you, obviously. You don't need to heap coals on their head when they are already struggling. Instead, ask them if they are feeling critical about themselves or if they have internalized the things you have requested already.

Most times, I find when a spouse can't hear anymore, it's because they feel flooded with critiques from the past already, their own or yours. In these seasons, it is imperative that you build your spouse up instead, complimenting them sincerely with what they are doing well, and prayerfully asking God, not them, for change for the next month or so. After this point, notice what has happened. Have they changed for the better with your consistent sincere compliments and prayers?

If not, bring this point to a counselor or coach who can help get you both unstuck more successfully than your negative comments probably will. Don't forget to give the building up time a good thirty days, so you can even the playing field more and your spouse, whom you love dearly, can find refreshment and be more ready for the changes you feel you need. Next, try the sandwich method.

For the spouse refusing change: Ask yourself why, if your spouse promises to use a loving format like the sandwich method to request change, can you not at least try to show them you hear them?

Remember, iron sharpens iron (Proverbs 27:17) and while spouses are helpers to one another, they are also supposed to be able to make requests and to be honest.

If you are so sensitive that your spouse does not feel safe to tell you when he or she feels an affront to the relationship or feels something between the two of you could be improved, you both lose. In marriage, you must be students of one another, learning the way your spouse feel loved best. This isn't a negative thing. Your spouse loves you if they are willing to work on the relationship, surely. And Someone loves you even more. God loves you just the way you are and He is willing to stand in the gap, defending you if an unfair request has been made. You don't need to fear that you won't be able to meet all of your spouse's needs, God already knows you can't. So let go of that false belief that if he or she heaps one more request for perfection upon you, you will topple. You won't, and yet you *can* try your best to love your spouse in his or her own love preferences.

Rest in the fact that you will never do it perfectly, that God loves you the way you are, but that trying to meet your spouse's desires and requests is a healthy part of marriage. If you cannot accept even requests of change using the sandwich method after considering this perspective, bring it to your counselor or coach for a more specific game plan. In the case of an abusive spouse, too many requests for change can be dangerous to one's self-worth.

ADDRESSING ANGER OUTBURSTS

Although some couples can make up with movie-star quality after a fiery ordeal, most couples that seek me out for help don't actually enjoy the making up process as much as they would actually like to avoid a fire-extinguisher-worthy battle in their marriage.

Typically, when one or both spouses have a bad temper that is easily riled up, someone in their life (often in childhood or early adulthood, or even the other person in this relationship) has allowed them to do this without setting a boundary. This pattern may have gotten a start as early as infancy. (Picture a mother cooing over a tantrumming toddler, which happens every day).

You do, in fact have your work cut out for you if someone has been permitted to both engage others like this and has received affirmation or coddling for having done so. If you are a spouse who often gets injured from your partner's anger outbursts, you are probably aware that trying many different angles can be very frustrating when none of them work.

You may even now be involved in a pattern of apologizing when someone else loses their temper even when you're not sorry since you don't want to have them get riled up too much, or especially in the case of feeling your own safety is at risk.

In the latter case, you need to run, not walk to your nearest domestic violence advocate and get help now since this endangers you and your family. There is never a time when it is okay or acceptable for a spouse to push or hit another, or to violently call you names. This is the exception to the rule when it comes to telling others about the battles and getting help, even if you don't start with a counselor but a caring friend or outside family member.

On the other hand, if you spouse is "just" getting upset, blaming, cajoling or emotionally manipulating you in fights, try communication tactics and being a scientist of the relationship to see what works as a first step. Do you push at someone and disrespect their boundaries when they are clearly agitated and need a cool down?

Someone who engages in anger outbursts may not have insight into what will help them but you can be a student of them, and try to talk it out with them when they are in a calm mode. Find out together what precipitated the outburst both generally and specifically? Were they exhausted? Did their boss make them feel badly? Are there any big red flags such as that they are not getting proper self-care?

Some people, when they feel emotionally threatened, have anger outbursts and they don't mean to hurt others, they are simply used to it and need someone else to set a boundary with them so they are forced to act differently.

Set a boundary with someone who has an uncontrolled anger outburst. Usually this means to refuse to talk to them until they both apologize and calm down. Don't compromise here. They won't like it, to be sure. But guess what? Life is about to get a little uncomfortable for them momentarily, which will bring increasing lasting and truer comfort than they have ever known.

If you are the one with an anger outburst issue, imagine having a very bad toothache and then being told a dentist was going to give you a shot and drill a larger hole in your tooth to fix the problem. At first, that sounds terrible but the lasting effect is pain-free bliss and before you know it, you are flossing with vigor and back to steak dinners and an occasional treat.

In marriage, when you truly fix anger outbursts, it will have a similarly joyous effect. Offended spouse need to confront the person before an outburst has taken place and say in front of a counselor, if possible,

"I realize you get your temper up when we fight, to the point of yelling and ... (whatever else they do). I don't mind if your voice rises a little since that's very normal but when you go off the handle and. (be specific), I have decided to walk away and try again later. I respect you and myself too much to be part of that any longer. I realize I may miss out on getting to the bottom of an important issues with you, so I will try other methods, such as resolving that when you are calm or speaking about it to a counselor or coach together. If you are not willing, I will talk to a counselor or mentor about my issues with you myself so I can figure out what to do. What I do know is that I can't be subject to fits of rage. We both know there are tips and tools to talk things out so we don't get to that point of escalation. If you are becoming escalated, let me know that. (Discuss a way to say it) and then I will back off. I make that commitment to you now, that knowing that you tend toward outbursts, if I see the following nonverbal signals (turning green like the Hulk, smoke coming out of your nose, and basically other signals, etc), I will say, "I see you are getting agitated from our fight. We can talk later, and for now, I'm going for a walk, going upstairs, etc. I love you."

In other words, set a boundary that also extends love and a chance to talk later. Your spouse feels threatened and is looking for control through the outburst so they need to be reassured of love as well as told they cannot do this to you.

BUILDING A BRIDGE

Sometimes there are issues that create a large divide between spouses, like a huge rushing river splitting the garden in irretrievable ways. Building a bridge across to your spouse is the only way for the connection to be attempted, and it takes work to build a solid bridge.

The bridge can look like compromises, exchanging ideas, coming across to your mate's side even when you don't want to or sometimes giving up your own way (Be prepared as this can sometimes look like big things, such as moving across the country for their dream job, or small things, such as going to their relative's home for dinner).

That bridge does need to be both built and crossed, time and time again in marriage, until it is just part of the beautiful landscape and the water. Then, and only then, can rippling passions or tensions below the surface become irrigating systems watering and nurturing the garden as you both move toward a flourishing marital garden.

A Christian counselor can help you to make the large decisions more strategically if you feel concerned because you feel like the only one crossing over, and *prayer* should be your first focus, before crossing any big bridges. Other ways of communication can get the life flowing back into the relationship but it begins with a bridge. When it's too hard, God is the master designer, so you can ask Him to help carry you across it when you really don't feel like doing something. If your conscience tells you not to compromise, postpone the decision until you have peace.

CONNECTION CUES

Communication doesn't always have to be about the negative disagreements either. Sit together and clear away your phone from distractions at least once per day. Allow yourselves the space to laugh, to sit and talk about things your spouse likes, as well as things you enjoy. Read his or her nonverbal communication messages to find cues that keep them interested in your and your topics. This is more thoroughly discussed in the *RELATE* book if you need further tips on being engaging in conversation.

Whatever you do, let some times just be for lighter topics. The Bible talks about how a spouse who nags is like a dripping and annoying leak (Proverbs 27:15), so steer clear of that kind of discussion, and stay focused on topics that are meaningful, fun, or light most of the time.

As Christian spouses, our conversations should not all be about ourselves and our drama and our pleasures. World topics, the Bible and others-focused communication should also be a regular part of your life together. <u>A morning devotional and prayer time is a good time for this to occur, even if it is hard to get up together.</u>

Is there a sick neighbor? Then don't gossip about it, talk about what the two of you may do to bring comfort or spend a moment praying. Is there a difficult boss? Again, spend time praying and help the other person to feel like you care and are a good listener for them. Make some long term and short terms goals together, even if they are simple ones like keeping a positive attitude. Don't be controlling over someone else's life stresses or work. Even though you are one flesh, your spouse is still another entity in their own right and has ideas and knowledge beyond yours about their job, although if properly timed, your influence can be strong. Prayerfully offer advice as needed, and try to honor and pray through each other's ideas for bringing change and light to the dark world.

> ***Love Note****: If you are discouraged about the way your spouse rejected your connection cues, don't give up after one or two tries. Imagine instead how it would feel if God gave up on you after one or two lost bids for your attention. How many times have birds chirped, skies been perfect, a gentle breeze crossed over you, a gorgeous sight lost in front of your distracted eyes, or a delicious smell wafting through the air without you spending a moment's time to even thank God? Millions probably and you have certainly misses some of your spouse's attempts also.*

No matter what, the bids for healthy connection you make with your spouse will be beautifully received by God who sees all and you too will bless you for your loving actions. Your spouse also will eventually realize that no one has ever loved them, save God, in the most special and honoring ways that you do.

SCHEDULE TIME TO COMMUNICATE

While some couples like to process conflict as it comes up, some couples need a daily, weekly, or monthly conversation about their issues since the issues are multiple, they have extremely busy schedules or their children are typically around. While it should involve the sandwich method and other respectful ways of strategizing, try to work toward only a monthly session of dealing with bigger conflicts, so your days and weeks can be full of light and life. If you need to hash things out daily or weekly, expect that you will have more draining conversation but the other side of the coin is that with more regular or natural conversations about conflict, you won't have to bottle things up for several weeks. Gauge your relationship preferences together, compromise and remember that as long as the two of you agree on how and when to talk things out, you can choose any timeframe!

After spending time learning to effectively communicate, Lexi put notes up around her house reminding her to think of good and pure thoughts (Phil 4:8) and to ask God for help in times of need (1 Peter 5:7). She realized these tangible reminders would be healthy ways for her to take ownership of her fast-thinking brain before everything just fell out of her mouth or she grew too anxious about her marriage.

She decided she would really think about the verse that words have the power of both death and life (Proverbs 18:21) and since she was the one who usually brought up conflict, that she would commit to choosing her conflict communication timing more carefully.

She enjoyed processing some of the lesser marital conflicts with her individual counselor as well as her friend who was a pastor's wife and a trusted confidant. These ways of releasing stress helped her to only bring what was necessary to Peter. Inevitably, she discovered that she was capable of letting go of more than she realized, the Thatchers became emotionally healthier as a couple from this simple act, especially since this pattern offered more life-giving space to the relationship. Lexi also decided that she would stop ignoring her husband's non-verbal signs of being overwhelmed when she verbally assaulted him on the phone, at work, and just when he came home. She tried to be a better listener, to take more deep breaths during conversations with him, and often to wait till the late evening, when her husband was freshest to really communicate.

She also realized that when her husband came home from work, she had erroneously thought he enjoyed getting all of the stressful topics out of the way right away so they could have a free and conflict-clear evening. Peter thought she was trying to bring up all of the stress just before he had a chance to let go of it, so he was coming home later and later and less and less patiently, because of this pattern. He was relieved to hear her intent was kindness and agreed to plan a time of day amenable to both of them for talking out the daily issues that needed addressing, such as bills, vacation time needed, dental visits to schedule, or chores to be divided more evenly.

Peter also had work of his own to do. Having come from a family where he had heard all of his life about women being annoying from his father (and from cultural depictions on television) as well as his own mother's incessant complaining during his childhood, he realized that he was annoyed with women before he even met Lexi.

He asked God for forgiveness and grace in releasing this previous belief to the best of his abilities. He decided to enter the home each day with life-giving qualities instead of checking sports scores on his phone or ignoring his wife to play with the children.

They decided this small amount of effort it took to bring Peter home from work better changed the whole evening dynamic. Peter worked hard to find fun, silly or meaningful ways to greet his wife, such as with an exuberant comment, a gentle and long lasting hug, a lingering kiss, a single rose, or just attention and a compliment toward his wife. "Hi, beautiful. The dinner smells wonderful." These small gestures that cost very little, brought his wife the reminder that her effort in creating a peaceful and lovely place for the family to spend time together was important and noticed. He in turn, released the stress that had been bottled up all day and his wife became someone he hurried to instead of dawdling.

Endnote:

DEALING WITH DIFFICULT CHILDREN OR STEPCHILDREN

This couple had equally intense children to deal with so they brought the kids in for a couple of mini-*RELEASE* sessions so they too could work toward a less chaotic life. The kids had a chance to spill their stress about their parents, which helped their counselor to understand the whole dynamic better. The children felt better having heard that their family was more secure now, and they were able to calm down emotionally since they often sabotaged their parents for attention.

If you have children, do not underestimate the fact that they notice the underlying tension between you since children's ability to pick up on stress and to act accordingly to ensure their own safely cannot be underestimated nor can they be blamed. It is important for you to assess whether your own children or stepfamily need a safe place to talk as you do the work of getting back on track. What are your final thoughts and resolutions on communication from this chapter? Spend a moment to journal and pray about this commitment.

_____

_____

_____

_____

Chapter 3

Leave the Past Behind

Matthew was seven years old when he first saw his father passed out from drinking. He was frightened to see his once-strong role model appear in such a weak and helpless state. Though his father kept a steady job, the instances of seeing him passed out drunk became normal eventually. Matthew spent weekends with his dad, learning implicitly that real men don't talk about stressful topics, but work hard during the week while letting loose with an excess of alcohol on the weekends. He vowed never to be like his dad, sensing the disorder it brought but an unhealthy view of stress-management had taken root deeply without his realizing it.

Matthew's wife Jenna had been raised by wealthy parents who coddled her and told her she deserved anything she ever wanted. At first, Matthew felt like he had won a prize by getting to marry such a privileged and special girl. However, he wasn't prepared for how she was used to having everything handed to her. She expected her husband to be the only breadwinner, especially after the children came. The pressures in their life mounted and things slowly began to unravel.

As their kids grew older, Matthew increasingly spent many weekends at his dad's house drinking, and Jenna meanwhile, found control by taking complete control of the family schedule and budget. She bought herself little luxuries frequently, giving Matthew a meager spending allowance, saying that he didn't make enough money for more.

Matthew increasingly relied on his dad's companionship and philosophy of life for alcohol and fun, and Jenna and Matthew began to lose their love as a couple, not surprisingly. Despite their early vows of eternal love through thick and thin, during stressful times in their marriage, they each clung to a past that had taught them unhealthy ways to cope with stress.

YOUR JOURNEY

Although your story may differ from Matthew and Jenna's, by now you've realized that no one enters their marriage without a past. At the onset of a relationship, most spouses don't realize just how much their old habits and family of origin behaviors have influenced them in the ways they live, both genetically and environmentally. Even if they do realize it a little, the fun of a brand new relationship may make the past seem unimportant or irrelevant, as couples embrace idealism in the early months or years of life together.

I have heard many people say, "I am not like my family of origin at all," at the beginning of marriage. Years later, they recognize that they are, in fact a lot like their families of origin, for better and sometimes for worse too. It's helpful for one to be able to step back and see this in order to bring changes that last. Do you think you are like your family of origin? Do you think your spouse is like his or hers? In which ways? Name some good and bad.

In more insightful relationships, one or both spouses recognize that their spouse carries difficulties from the past into the current marriage even at the beginning. These same people often secretly believe their love will be enough to change their spouse. When that doesn't happen, it can be downright discouraging.

"He won't drink once he sees how well I can meet his needs," or "She flirts but once she is able to confirm my love for her with a marriage union, she won't," or "She does whatever her mother says, but once we are married, she will stop and consider me first," are some of the more flamboyant comments I hear from engaged and newly married couples.

If these were your thoughts at the onset of your relationship, you may be chuckling (or groaning) now at your early naïveté. If you aren't yet married, you may be hopeful and that is good, but he realistically hopeful and wise!

And as you know, marriage at its best *can* help you through addictions and unhealthy boundaries with others, reduce or eradicate tendencies to adultery, giveyous freedom from an unhealthy family of origin and much more. *But* just because someone gets married, they are still human, still flawed, and still shaped by their culture and past, despite every intention of good.

In this chapter, I will help you to say farewell to the unhealthy habits of your past by taking more practical and intentional steps. Just don't assume difficult habits and spiritual bondage issues will fall off like scales without work. Pruning is a job and it's yours if you want a thriving marital garden.

So, since in the last chapters you learned about how your previous ideas of both rest and communication influence your marriage in profound ways, we will consider some of your historical markers in life that have done the same thing, both in your marital past but also in your childhood and your adult unmarried past.

As a quick exercise, check the box next to each of the items you were influenced by in your past. Even if you believe the influence was minimal, check off all the items you have experienced.

DIFFICULT MOMENTS ON THE JOURNEY

___Emotional abuse (including manipulation).
___Sexual abuse.
___Physical abuse.
___Loss of a close friend or family member.
___Have or had a parent with an addiction.
___Failed out of school.
___Got suspended from work or school.
___Got caught in pornography.
___Imprisonment.
___Having an affair.
___Military or job-related trauma.
___Job loss(es).
___Illness or mental health crisis.
___Loss of a child or miscarriage.

___Breaking up with someone you had been intimate with either through marriage or divorce (or cohabiting with).
___Other difficult issues (specify):

_____

Although you may feel completely separated from any one of these events, it's almost impossible not to let such big issues affect you. Experiencing any one of these instances above can contribute to a lack of thriving in marriage, even if it occurred many years prior to your union. If so, this is almost certainly robbing you of your current marital satisfaction, especially if you are not intentionally releasing this old baggage.

Letting go of the past involves a healing journey to a new place, a 'promised land' of marital and personal peace. God spoke to His people from the beginning of time, and a theme for all of us since has been that if we acknowledge our weaknesses, throw away everything that hinders and love God and others well, we will have an abundant life. This is what I mean by a marital promised land. It is yours for the taking if you do your very best to follow this lead!

As you explore your own past a bit more analytically, write down some of your own (not your spouse's) needs for healing from these earlier mentioned times of your life. Was there a difficult first marriage you still hold resentment from? Did you have a parent emotionally or physically abuse you that you never forgave or released shame from? Did you feel wounded by your spouse in a way that has left you scarred? Take time to write down some of the emotional baggage you are or may be carrying around, at least to a small degree.

_____
_____
_____
_____

COMMITTING TO HEAL

Take heart if you have listed one or more than one item in the previous section of difficulties. Just as there is always a reason when a garden fails to thrive such as from lack of light or refreshment, there is also always a reason when a marriage fails to thrive. In this chapter, we need to uncover that. Scars and difficult foundations have been laid from imperfect families of origin on both sides, many of whom had the best of intentions but just operated out of their own spaces of pain and survival, never reaching their own marital promised land. *Healing is possible even when this is the case.* God's protection, provision, and direction are available for the road back to marital health.

As we frame this healing process as a journey, remember that while you may not be going anywhere physically, a retreat of some sorts, even if at home, will be important. Whether it be aforementioned time set-aside time with a counselor, a regular and extensive journaling time, time with an accountability partner or mentor, or a regularly and focused prayer time, you will need a place to process.

If you need some time to get away and take a marital retreat, I recommend either doing a marital intensive at our office with one of our trained professionals, or visiting a well-respected national marriage intensive, such as Caring for the Heart (caringfortheheart.com) Ministries in Colorado Springs, which is a donation-based intensive journey focused on healing and heart issues from a supportive and wise Christian framework.

Wherever your journey takes place, you'll need to move out of the current marital position you are stuck in and venture out into the great unknown.

When you are sick, you know that healing takes time and good self-care measures, and you intuitively know to take time to rest, to follow the doctor's orders, and when necessary, to take medicines.

Newly diagnosed diabetes patients will drastically alter their diets, counting even the smallest of calories, those with high blood pressure will cut out unhealthy fats, and those with migraines will search earnestly for triggers.

Similarly, those with marriage difficulties who truly want healing will become better students of themselves and their spouses, will work hard, and will commit to understanding more about their own dynamic.

Next are a few potential areas that hurt your marriage, either directly or indirectly. These areas of life need to be both acknowledged and released squarely for true healing to take place. They cannot and must not be taken into the future. There is no shame or judgment from me passed to you if you do something on this list. I don't condemn you any more than Jesus condemned the woman in an extramarital relationship. But like Him, I acknowledge that in order to find healing, you must, as He put it, "Go now and leave your life of sin." (John 8:11). Jesus knows that however unhealthy methods of coping seem to help heal the short-term physical or emotional pain, clinging to them for any length of time will only cause more thorny setbacks in the long-term.

RECOGNIZE UNHEALTHY COPING MECHANISMS
(Circle all of the ones you have done in the past six months)

- Not overeating.
- Drinking too much alcohol.
- Yelling at your family.
- Hurting another person physically.
- Controlling your spouse.
- Exercise addiction.
- Masking the pain via gossip
- Masking the pain via narcissism (excessive interest and attention in one's self or appearance).
- Binge eating.
- Emotional affairs.
- Fantasies, even "mild" ones.
- Pornography.
- Flirting.
- Pain pills.

If you saw one or more things on the list that you do to receive pleasure, it may be hard to admit it. You will almost surely justify things you do to compensate for the lack of love in your marriage by saying, "This was the only thing getting me by." If this is true, that this thing or these things are holding you up and strengthening you right now, why are you still working on healing your marriage? It's because these things *haven't* done the job. Darkness, by definition, cannot bring light and light and darkness cannot have fellowship. (2nd Cor 6:14). This crutch is actually tearing your marriage apart, make no mistake.

Relying on any of these coping mechanisms is more like putting a band-aid over a shotgun wound than a real healing agent. You need true mending, something only God can give, which is ultimately deeper and a more full solution than these temporary and unhealthy fixes.

Ask yourself this, especially if you don't know if you plan to let go of this other relationship or negative lifestyle choice. Are you truly peaceful and joyful? Are you thriving maritally? Physically? Are your children living the *best* life they can under your parentage? Do you think you are pleasing God? Are these the things you dreamed of doing for self-care when you were at your best or a small child?

GETTING GOD'S HELP

If the answer is no to any one of those questions, you need to let these things go for healing to take place, and to realize that God Himself, not you, nor any lovers, addictions, or even your spouse can fully fill the void that these things are trying to fill. This is why all twelve-step groups are based upon a belief in God.

ACCEPTING CHRIST

In order to heal, *ask Jesus into your heart for the first time or as a reconnection time.* Tell God that you understand your sins, realize that He is the only bridge to a new life, and ask Him to be your Savior so you can enjoy regular fellowship with Him, to have His Holy Spirit inside of you, and to receive the gift of eternal life. God loves you and He will help you more than anyone on this journey. Don't delay this wonderful relationship! As John 3:16 says, "For God so loved the world that He gave His one and only Son, that whoever believes in Him shall not perish but have eternal life."

Rekindle or begin your journey by reading your Bible, finding a church family to become a part of, and attending a small group at a church in order to get to know Him better through His body! See a pastor, a counselor or a coach for help in this matter, or make a regular appointment with your Christian mentor. As a reminder, a mentor should be someone who shares your values and cares about your marriage, as well as seems older or wiser in these areas, not just a friend to gab with.

CREATING GOOD HABITS

In the process of releasing the past, we know from Scripture that as we release sin, we must simultaneously add things in, since an idle mind will only make us long for more sin and darkness if we don't fill it with good (Matthew 12:43-45). Ask God how you can stay busy and also get healthy amounts of refreshment in between. Rest assured, God will keep you busy enough for His kingdom so you are able to resist these intense longings fully even if it's hard at first. One especially important Scripture to remember is that God says, "No temptation has overtaken you but such as is common to man; and God is faithful, who will not allow you to be tempted beyond what you are able, but with the temptation will provide the way of escape also, so that you will be able to endure it"(1st Corinthians 10:13, *NASB*).

BEST SUPPORT STAFF

We can also become stronger as we let go of difficult habits by bringing our spouse on board as our primary support team member. Let he or she in on the plans you have made and ask them to cheerlead for you! Spouses, remember not to gossip about your spouse as they walk through this fire of letting go and trying to be obedient to God. This takes courage and will likely make them more sensitive as they let go (think caffeine headache times ten!).

Watch out for people who don't want to empathize but simply to criticize your spouse along the way (now, or ever). Pray together that you would be there to protect one another's emotions from well-meaning (or ill-wishing) relatives and friends who want to contribute to helping in the family struggle. Help your spouse to know that they are your first priority, and make sure you are "leaving and cleaving" (Gen 2:24) family of origin so they know you are to be trusted while they work things out and will give only mutually decided upon information to outside family members. It is usually better to talk to an outside mentor if you need to process your reaction to your spouse's emotions since they aren't as emotionally wired to protect or defend you as your own family of origin.

Prayerfully, a couple who comes together well may even decide to confront an extended family issue together, but if so, do this with patience and wisdom and whenever possible, with the help of a trusted mentor.

EASY DOES IT

Just because you acknowledge that this is a healing season, you still want and need fun, beauty, emotional support, painlessness, and romance, right? Try to be patient, as all of these things are far more likely to happen when you are allowing God to heal your pain His way. This means naturally and without the sinful outlets of addictions so it is okay if life is a little bland or hard for a while. Still, it is vital to draw out a schedule for yourself that involves staying busy with healthy stress-relieving outlets in between work and enjoying healthy rewards for progress. If you haven't already done so, take time now to make an appointment with someone who can hold you accountable for the healing journey.

***Love Note to Spouses of Someone Letting Go of Major Addictions:** You need help in healing so please make sure you ask for the help and partnership of one of two friends who love and care for you. Do not, I repeat, do not, treat your spouse like a baby who needs to be controlled. Support him or her like an adult. Don't be codependent. You do not need a parent-child relationship with your spouse and it won't endear you to one another if you behave like either one of those roles. Set your personal boundaries and keep them firmly in place during the healing process. Give them plenty of gentle and patient love without sacrificing your self-worth, and your life with God. Do not tolerate abuse of any kind. Just remember, don't ditch someone taking genuine steps toward healing. Remember 1st Cor 13 and keep moving ahead! Balance is key. Speaking the truth in love is also key (Ephesians 4:15). Support groups like Celebrate Recovery, Al-Alon, and small groups at your church are wonderful ways to get connected with healthy support!*

FORGIVENESS & RELEASING RESENTMENT

Now that we have ascertained that you have had at least some pain in your past (even if you are not a full-blown addict), and have allowed at least some unhealthy coping mechanisms to make you less than satisfied in your life, it's time to see if there is anything else right here and now holding you back. This is an important time to remember that forgiveness is part of God's plan.

First, remember that we can never fully judge another human being properly. Although you may know someone's current situation well enough to make a modest assessment about his or her behavior (such as when it's your own toddler getting into the cookie jar - if only all situations were that clear-cut!), it isn't helpful for you to try to play God in another adult's life. Therefore, since you cannot see the generational sin in their family history perfectly, have not lived their adult life, don't have their genetic makeup or exact blueprints, nor can you otherwise fully put yourselves in their shoes, you must release them and yourself from the binding and dark power of unforgiveness. It just isn't fair to pretend you could do things differently if you were them.

Thankfully, we serve a just God who sees all and *can* handle judgment all by Himself. And He, knowing all things, calls for forgiveness. He doesn't want you to hold resentment, although there is a time for confronting. Maybe you felt hurt, and in the earlier part of this book you realized a family member or friend had wounded you more than you had realized. Pray over God's perfect timing in confronting and/or releasing that person, and use Matthew 18:15-16 as a guideline for approaching them if you need to. Don't gossip about it, that won't bless you or anyone else. Instead, Jesus commands, (not asks) us to forgive others. This doesn't mean resisting masking, stuffing, or acknowledging hurt. Instead, here are some instructions on forgiving.

HOW TO FORGIVE

In order to forgive well, you must do the following;

1. First acknowledge before God that you have been hurt. Sometimes you also feel called to address the other person. No spouse can make this choice for one another. Do what God is telling you to do.
2. You must clearly pray, "I choose to forgive this person for the wrongdoing they have done me." If you feel you have widespread unforgiveness, take an entire month to let God

know you are choosing to forgive anyone who has wronged you, intentionally or unintentionally.

3. When negative actions, attitudes, or feelings come up against this person again, repeat steps one and two.

4. Pray the prayer Jesus asked us to pray on a daily basis also (Matthew 6:9-13).

5. If you are harboring unforgiveness for yourself, make sure you acknowledge that and give yourself the same grace you gave to others at each of the previous four steps.

6. If someone keeps offending you, how often do you forgive? The Bible said seventy times seven (Matthew 18:22). In case you are slow to catch on, it means continue this forever, because God forgave us of much more than anyone else could ever do against us.

7. Remember, forgiveness does not acknowledge that anyone was in the right when they wounded another, it only releases the offended person and the offender from the hate that accompanies unforgiveness, and it frees the offended person of unnecessary baggage in their healing journey. Most of all it encourages the forgiving person to be in right relationship with God, who commands us to forgive in all cases and says that if we obey Him, we will receive many blessings (Deuteronomy 28).

Forgiving also includes forgiving those who have not asked for forgiveness, which is surprising to some. Nowhere in the Bible does it say not to forgive if someone does not ask you specifically. No, forgiving is an intentional act of releasing yourself and the other person of the embittered revenge you feel they may deserve in some way. It says, "I may not trust you, I may still have to give a consequence or make a change in our relationship as a result of your action, but I love you and will continue to be faithful to God who calls me to love and to forgive you. I release my unforgiveness and let God be the ultimate judge."

Here is a copy of the Lord's Prayer for those who are not familiar with it. When his disciples asked Jesus how they should pray, He told them to pray the following (and forgiveness is implied),

PRAY

The Lord's Prayer (Matthew 6:9-13).

"Our Father in heaven,
Hallowed (holy) be Your name,
Your kingdom come,
Your will be done,
on earth as it is in heaven.
Give us today our daily bread.
And forgive us our debts,
as we also have forgiven our debtors.
And lead us not into temptation,
but deliver us from the evil one.

WHO TO FORGIVE
(Whom do you need to forgive right now? Do it!)

_____
_____
_____
_____

Make the commitment to forgive this person or people as many times as is necessary. Pray the Lord's Prayer on a daily basis to remind you of the ways to love God best, which includes forgiveness.

Finally, don't cast your pearls (best gifts) before swine (toxic people) (Matthew 7:6). Instead, refuse to continue a relationship that is completely destructive. Don't keep placing yourself in the line of abuse. It's time to set boundaries with people who are manipulative and unhealthy, so that you don't find yourself in the line of offense again and again. Use common sense. If this person is your spouse, then you will need focused time and wisdom for God's miracles before taking drastic measures such as walking away.

Walk through this difficult season with Christian accountability so you will know if separation or divorce should be considered in extreme cases. It should not be recommended lightly since God makes certain concessions for it (Matthew 19:7-9) but says He hates divorce (Malachi 2:16). Outside of marriage, use common sense also. Don't keep going to hang out with a best friend who is horrible to you or allow a parent to bully or use you now that you are a grown up. You couldn't help it then but there is no excuse now!

> **Love Note**: *Let this statement sink in:*
> *Forgiveness involves showing both mercy and wisdom.*

In the *Attach Well* chapter you will have a chance to visit some more in-depth ways spouses have wounded one another so that after you have forgiven, you can still address lingering hurts in your relationship. Knowing this, don't wait to offer forgiveness for the past offenses in and for all things now!

WALKING THROUGH THE DESERT

Even if you have a supportive spouse or a great team of friends who are encouraging you to let go of a bad habit from your past or present life, you almost always find that after you have walked away from the sin that was entangling you, you are still waiting for new growth and new patterns to settle in. Usually in this time, there are temptations. Satan has taken particular notice of your vulnerable positioning; you have released resentments and are walking away from bad habits. What that really says about you is that you are becoming ripe for ministry. This is when Satan attacks, of course, since if you are already entangled, he is usually pretty happy to see you send yourself into a downward spiral. Now you are a real threat and the war is just beginning.

TEMPTATIONS IN THE DESERT

Another way of viewing this new season of life is to describe it as a time in a bleak desert of sorts, when you aren't yet to your promised land of healthy relating and you have doubts about ever getting there or doubts about God's provision for the journey. The Israelites, as Moses led them out of slavery in Egypt felt the same and they sinned in their wanderings and remained in that desert place for *forty years* (Numbers 32:13).

Most of them never made it to the new and wonderful land for their bitter complaining and lack of faith kept them back from God's favor. Joshua and Caleb did make it, however, and had a wonderful adventure and an amazing victory that is still celebrated today as one of the greatest acts and rewards for godly obedience of all time. (Joshua 1:5).

Jesus can relate to the desert season also (Matthew 4:1-11). Just as He was about to unleash His incredible ministry, Jesus, by the power of the Holy Spirit, went immediately to the desert where He was tempted by the devil. He was fasting and spending time preparing for His ministry in this season. Because of this, He resisted *all* pressure and in fact, used God's word (the Bible) to refute every temptation Satan laid out (Mark 1:13).

In the same way, we are tempted when we are planning and preparing to do God's work. We have prayerfully been released into our ministries and into a healthy marriage, but when temptation or doubt (tools of darkness) hit, we often quickly fall into the trap designed by Satan to snag us.

Remember, use healthy coping tools, especially God's word to resist in this time. This will help you to move through it as quickly as possible, since after a time of faithfulness and putting one foot in front of the other, the new habits will replace the old and the temptations will release their firm grip on you. Tell the Lord when you need Him to give you extra help during the most difficult moments. Wait to hear His still, small, but deeply encouraging response.

Just suppose you and your spouse commit to doing better in your marriage, you are very excited about your new plans, and then all of the sudden, a fight ensues. Your spouse makes you feel that empty feeling from your past, the one that represents fear, aloneness, doubt and vulnerability. Instead of going to God for direction in this desert moment, you instead allow the darkness, the old ways, to fill up your thought life.

"Since she doesn't seem to want to help me, I think I'll have another drink. I gave that up for her and she didn't even care!" or "He doesn't care about me after all. I guess mom was right. I'm going to go tell her all about it and she will bring the comfort I have been seeking. So will a good old-fashioned spending spree. I deserve it."

Maybe the temptations are subtler. Your mind allows itself to wander to thoughts about someone at work or church or who seems satisfied with you just the way you are. Maybe you don't think about another person directly, but now you feel you have permission to look at pornography, to go into your closet and overeat, to lie in bed not doing anything, or otherwise allow evil to triumph.

This is dangerous. God has something better for you. Much better. Goals are still before you in those awful moments, just as Jesus' were. In fact, during Jesus' desert moment, His entire known ministry was still before him. I believe you too, have an entire ministry before you as well. What do you think that might be?

_____

_____

_____

_____

THE ONLY WAY OUT

When Jesus followed this winning formula of using God's Word to refute Satan, see what happened. Instead of pausing to even allow Satan's comments to sink in, (which involved questioning God, of course) in Matthew 4:1-11, Jesus combats the devil with these Scriptures smoothly, "Then Jesus said to him, "Go, Satan! For it is written, 'You shall worship the Lord your God, and serve Him only.' Then the devil left Him; and behold, angels came and began to minister to Him."

When you also choose to soak up God's word and live for and in Him, you can resist every temptation and will have angels ministering to you, as we know from Hebrews 1:14, "Are they not all ministering spirits, sent forth to minister for them who shall be heirs of salvation? *(KJV)*" and Psalm 91:11 "For He shall give His angels charge over thee, to keep thee in all thy ways *(KJV)*."

If you cling to God in these difficult times, you'll see that these weeds of lust, rage, jealousy, and other damaging habits bring a choking death and not life. You will see that only following God brings true life. The other desires become almost laughable as you realize that you lose all over again by choosing any one of these temporary and harmful fillers of your soul.

If Jesus had clung to doubt, fear, anger or unforgiveness toward God, rejecting His divine destiny that did involve trials after all, His ministry would have been thwarted. Jesus could have chosen to rule as a rich king while He was here on earth for short-term glory but He instead chose the nails and to suffer for our sin for *our* ultimate good.

Let's face it, nails (and trials) hurt. And sometimes, choosing the right thing hurts. Don't be afraid of the hurt you feel from mini-rejections which is what you feel when you have a marital spat. Cry as needed. Let the hurt wash over you and then allow God to heal you fully with His truth and with the body of Christ who, in dark times in your marriage, can remind you of who you are in Him.

If you choose to continue to think about choosing the sinful things from your past, you are only holding yourself back, as well as the others you influence. On the other hand, your darkest moments will become part of your testimony if you walk forward into the light of Christ. Prayerfully ask God for the pure and holy road to follow Him. Allow Him to take the lead, letting Him know you need His help.

_____

_____

_____

_____

If you think you don't have control over your mind for the battle, take comfort in 2nd Corinthians 10:5 that you do, "We demolish arguments and every pretension that sets itself up against the knowledge of God, and *we take captive every thought to make it obedient to Christ* "(emphasis added).

RELEASING IDOLS

One continual problem many people have when they leave the prior enslavement and take the journey to get to the Promised Land is that they take idols along. Idols are anything symbolic that have at some point or another, been a substitute for God in your life. In the Bible, there are many times when actual idols were carved out and worshipped. Taking idols along, even if they aren't metal figurines, still happens today, though in different ways. This is a dangerous sabotage of all of your goals so I encourage you to do whatever it takes to drop them.

Tell your spouse first if there are idols you may be tempted to bring along, since darkness has no power when it is revealed in the light.

This may sound hard but marriage needs honesty to thrive. If you just aren't feeling like you can share about this "idol" of sorts in the marriage, then it's time to talk to someone who mentors you about what that is. If you are already working with a counselor or coach directly as you read this, then it's time for you to be honest about the need for real accountability as you let go of these idols.

WHAT ARE YOU CARRYING?

Maybe you have taken a step back and in terms of your gambling or work ethic or anger outbursts are on the right track now. However, you still carry a secret marriage-killing idol such as one of the aforementioned issues like pornography, deceit, an emotional affair or a spending issue.

Another subtle idol is control. Women carry this from the Garden of Eden and it hurts a marriage just as much as man's pride ever did because it is abusive to try to control sometimes entirely. It also demoralizes or discourages them.

If however, you don't acknowledge idols for what they are to yourself as well as to someone else, especially to your spouse but also another accountability partner, you are still silently preventing yourself from doing your part to make this marriage wonderful, and you really can't expect any of the tools to work.

Believe me, your spouse will eventually know deep down you aren't loving them from the heart. They may stay by your side and love you faithfully as you go through this crisis, but wouldn't you rather not be going through it? Wouldn't you rather thrive? Carrying idols won't bring this. It only increases the risk of losing your spouse. I know you don't what that, deep down. Talk about the troubling issues that have left such deep scars in your marriage and choose to drop everything holding you back!

Ask yourself and one another which idols you are still carrying into your marriage? Write them down here.

_____

_____

_____

_____

How do you feel about carrying these idols knowing if you continue to carry them you have one guarantee. *You will never reach the marital promised land.*

_____

_____

_____

_____

Don't let your marital promised land wait another day. Let go of those idols, drop them in the desert sand where they belong forever and walk forward more lightly and free of the enslavement.

Now, take some time to think, talk or write about this and to prayerfully commit to leaving the idols behind. Don't continue this journey until you have done so.

_____

_____

_____

_____

TAKING ONLY WHAT IS NEEDED

When God sent the Israelites out of Egypt, He told them to let go of everything that enslaved them, but they were to bring some important memorials. (Exodus 13:19). Although we want to leave idols behind, we have certain good qualities we have picked up throughout hardships that we definitely want to carry forward. Don't leave behind wonderful traits from your family of origin or helpful tools you learned in your first marriage or relationship. If your mother was abusive but she taught you to clean up after yourself, hold that healthy tension with being thankful for what you learned positively from her, and enjoy that she taught you some wonderful skills, even if the abuse was difficult.

Maybe you drink (or drank) a lot and are giving that up now but you also have a very good work ethic. Don't rob Peter to pay Paul in this time, and stop working hard or become a glutton, now slacking, cutting corners and otherwise being lazy. No, take that wonderful work ethic on with you, and also remember to rest and to celebrate well also!

Many times we can decide that we have cut off a certain person or time period in our lives without realizing that not only were we shaped negatively, but we were also grown, refined and matured in some other ways by that person or experience. These attributes are very important to our natures and our marriages. Spend a moment thinking about what traits you learned from the past, whether in this marriage or before this marriage, that you don't want to leave behind as you walk forward. If you have children from a previous relationship, carry the love and bond you share with them proudly forward also. They need you more than ever now that you are becoming a healthier example to them of God's love and faithfulness. What will you commit to carrying forward?

_____

_____

_____

_____

REACHING THE PROMISED LAND - CELEBRATING WELL

As you get into the new patterns of behaving in healthier ways and letting go of the sin that so easily entangles, you will find that your new life has freedom and joy like never before. Don't forget the celebration markers!

These small and large acts of celebration includes getting proper rest with your spouse as you learned in Chapter One and effectively communicating like you learned in Chapter Two. They can also include defining ceremonies, special meals or parties, or simple daily exercises in small segments! The biggest reasons for celebrating, however are that you renewed your relationship with God and began to trust Him as you let go of sin in this chapter. It is now time to move forward to embrace your spouse in a deeper way than ever before. Having let go of the pain of the past, it is time to make sure your attachment to one another is sealed intimately as well. We will talk about this in next chapter! For now, enjoy a moment with Matthew and Jenna from this chapter to witness how they healed together.

Matthew and Jenna had been married for fourteen years when they hit the aforementioned wall of despair. After they had some good counseling however, Matthew learned to more directly address Jenna's damaging overspending, instead of passive aggressively going to his dad for an emotional or monetary bailout. If you remember, this was rooted in a lack of understanding of a male's role as a Christian husband as well as in his longing for his emotional father figure needs to be met, since they weren't when he was a child.

By facing this hard truth as well as Matthew's drinking and Jenna's overspending together, they stopped the bad habits that were holding them back from the promised land. Matthew both admitted to and stopped gossiping to his dad about Jenna and got into a support group to get a handle on his out of control weekend drinking.

Jenna admitted to spending excessively and exercising control to find safety in the storms of Matthew's withdrawal. Jenna and Matthew together worked on a budget that would allow for self-care, rest, better communication, and letting go of their negative past influences.

Instead of stopping and letting those be the only lesson learned however, this couple reached their marital promised land in the process by hanging on to what was good and what they had learned during the difficult season. Jenna had learned that her husband was passive-aggressive because he had no power or freedom to grow up well. When Jenna neglected to discuss financial and other decisions with him, he felt powerless and sad and chose to drink since he was completely overwhelmed. But on the positive side, since they were tighter on money than she had been as a child, Jenna also learned that she knew how to budget. She also got a small part time job so she could enjoy a few luxuries since she was used to those and preferred to continue small amounts of pampering herself.

Matthew realized that going to his dad helped as a temporary fix, but didn't make him feel better in the ways of being a strong provider. It made him feel weak and like a child again, begging for his dad's attention and approval. He admitted that he didn't feel either deep down, even after all of these years. As he sobered up, he brought a stronger insistence upon a say in the family schedule and budget into their healthier dynamic, and realized that even though the drinking was difficult to let go of, it was not impossible. He chose not to gossip about his marriage anymore either, since it made him feel directly worse about himself and his choice to marry Jenna, making the temptation to drink that much stronger.

As a result of these positive choices, this couple reached their marital promised land. Jenna said, "I see now that Matthew has some great ideas and he deserves a voice in our budget and family plans. I am learning to trust him again now that he isn't checking out on weekends with alcohol. Also, I was annoyed that Matthew depended on his dad for everything and when I got a job, it taught me that I could take care of myself, which helped me to have more self-respect and afforded me some of my former luxuries such as manicures occasionally as well as gifts for the kids.

It also helped me to set boundaries with Matthew about his drinking now that I'm not so codependent (or 'unhealthily tied to his issues'). Now that Matthew is not drinking at all, we are not talking about our marriage to his parents or mine and we are not being silent about our finances together. We are laughing more together too, planning fun things to do with the extra money in our pockets, and more committed than ever not to let temporarily but ultimately empty pleasures steer us off track again. We renewed our vows last September, lead a marriage Bible study at church, and have been going strong ever since."

This couple was definitely not perfect, but they didn't carry the old follies forward as you can see. Instead, the gems that had come out of that refining furnace of trial were carried on to bless the marriage and this couple was thriving now more than ever, even though they let go of almost everything that had previously seemed to matter so much.

BE PATIENT

Remember, you are letting go and haven't yet seen a flourishing garden, yours will look patchy for awhile. That's how any garden looks when plants are newly growing and being dug up. Life and gardens are just messy from time to time and in certain seasons. This is especially true when compared to other gardens that have been well tended to for many years by prior generations with love, care and wisdom.

Don't be discouraged then, if others people's marriages seem easier. If you do not see all the fruit now, you may be a family who plants new seeds and enjoys some early growth instead. Rest assured, God will bless your healthy efforts and future generations upon whom your influence will reap both the fruit and the harvest.

Remember Moses, who as wonderful, special and anointed as he was, only got to gaze from afar at the Promised Land (Deuteronomy 34) since his sin was so offensive to God. However, his younger family actually got to benefit and be able to live there. If you feel like Moses, old and withering on the outside with little chance for an amazing life, although new and fresh in your healthy attitudes, don't let go of your dreams to have it all. God can cleanse you, free you of sin, and allow you to save others from the same brokenness you have lived out for so many years. Plus, you too will be saved in countless ways!

Chapter 4

Embrace Sexual Intimacy

As you become healthier together, it's time to think about touch and sexual intimacy in your marriage. Likely if you have hit some rough spots in your marriage, the intimate moments in the bedroom aren't always ideal either. This is because, of course, intimacy is about more than just time in the bedroom. In this chapter, we will discuss both sexual and non-sexual touch, as well as help you to release some unhealthy attitudes or practices in your emotional and sexual life. You will also learn several practical tools to release sexual tension and to connect with the love of your life!

On a Tuesday night when the kids were finally asleep and Chris was just getting up from story time, Lana whispered seductively into her husband's ear, "I want to show you something in the bedroom in a little while."

Chris was happy to hear this and he decided to wait for her to call him in to show him what she meant. He waited for about ten minutes before heading into the room, locking the door to their bedroom suite behind him. There was soft music on and he could hear talking. She was on the phone with her sister. Oh no, he thought.

"I'll be right there, ok?" she mouthed, covering the phone and shooing him off. She had hair removal cream on her legs and eyebrows and her hair was wet from a shower. She also had mascara dripping down her cheeks. Still, an invitation was an invitation and he was really looking forward to some much-needed intimate time with his wife.

Chris waited on the couch in the living room, playing with his phone and just hoping things would head in the right direction in a few minutes. About thirty minutes later, Lana walked up to him in her beautiful silky nightgown, her damp hair up, hair remover cream rinsed off, and mascara off of her cheeks.

"Honey, are you asleep?" she said to her husband, gently shaking him. He was so exhausted he didn't even hear her. She sighed. This kind of thing happened more than she'd like to admit, without a kiss goodnight, without a prayer, and without sexual fulfillment for either spouse. The two of them went to bed at separate times and her leading sexual promise had been made void yet again.

Since this is a simple example, we can easily see some of this couple's flaws and even patterns. Chris checks out on his phone not trying to do anything particular to romance his wife, and Lana makes Chris wait. Chris didn't wait up for her, but lie down and let her do everything. Lana did very little to set the tone. Ideally, what could they have done differently? Their sexual style lacked intention, obviously but what else? Spend a moment journaling out some ideas you might try if you were in their shoes.

_____

_____

_____

_____

Here is one way their situation could have had a happier ending,

1. Lana whispered the same whisper into her husband's ear, a sultry and intoxicating invitation that was specific, "Wait for me on the bed, lock the door, and smell handsome, baby."
2. Chris made the bed, poured a glass of water or wine, took a quick shower or dabbed some cologne on, turned some soft piano music on and for good measure, lit a candle and brought a silky blanket out of the closet.
3. Lana, meanwhile, was putting her hair in a simple but stylish manner, making sure she smelled feminine and accentuated her body with lingerie or taking all or most of her clothes off.

4. Chris, after about five minutes, could knock at the bathroom door and let his wife know he was eager for her. He could straighten up the bedroom while waiting versus lying on the couch thinking of sports scores or Facebooking. He could leave his phone out of the room altogether or put it on silent and place it far away.

5. They could start intimacy then or simply ease into it if they needed connection time first, talking about non-stressful topics or massaging one another. This sounds simple but definitely more fun than what ensued and from start to finish, would have taken only the twenty or thirty minutes it took for her to get off the phone and for him to fall asleep.

While Chris and Lana's situation may sound obvious to you, sometimes your own situation may not feel so simple. And as you bring not only sexual issues into the relationship but also personality differences, fatigue, family of origin issues and even past sexual relationship styles in, your bedroom can become pretty crowded!

THE IMPORTANCE OF TOUCH

Before we can talk about your sexual intimacy further (I know some of you are especially eager for this conversation and you are almost there!), we need to get back to the basics. Touch. Touch is an intrinsic need for all of humanity. Simply put, without touch, we die. Maybe not right away or physically, since as adults we have all passed the precarious state of infanthood where tried and true failure to thrive from neglect does indeed lead to physical death. However, without touch, there is a death of sorts for everyone and whether you are married or single, making touch part of your world will help you to thrive!

With this in mind, what is your favorite non-sexual way to receive touch? A hug? A back scratch?

_____

_____

_____

_____

Although most people don't stop to consider it, sometimes a bad mood, a sad feeling or a relationship issue that seems huge at the time can be mended with some good old-fashioned simple non-sexual touch. Meeting that basic need of humanity can go a long way and even if it feels like it, asking your spouse to touch you non-sexually is not a strange request. Take a moment to write down several ways *you* enjoy non-sexual touch and when it could perhaps improve your mood? Share it with your spouse also at home or in your next session!

_____

_____

_____

_____

If your spouse won't provide non-sexual loving touch to you, you can still make sure to get it from another healthy method such as a gentle loofah in the tub, hot baths, massages at a massage studio, rubbing tense muscles, brushing hair softly, giving hugs to your friends, etc. Write your ideas here.

_____

_____

_____

_____

If you'd like to enjoy more physical touch with one another and don't know where to begin, here is a short list of the ways you can offer physical touch to and from one another;

- Massages
- Back scratches
- Sexual activity
- Holding hands
- Hugging
- Kissing
- Baths or showers together, washing one another
- Arms intertwined
- Arms around each other while sitting
- Slow dancing
- Placing an arm on someone during conversation
- Caressing
- Tickling one another

As a beginning, try doing at least one of these loving touches everyday minimally, with the upward goal of three acts of loving (non-sexual) touch per day. Before you get overwhelmed, remember that a quick hug and kiss before or after work are part of quality touch, as is the simple act of putting your arm around your spouse while you watch a TV program. Though this kind of touch doesn't dazzle, it speaks quiet volumes about safety and commitment to one another non-verbally.

LOST IN EDEN

When God created male and female, He also made plans for them to have sexual intimacy, calling them to be fruitful. In the biblical book of Song of Songs, we read about the sensual and fragrant metaphors of grapes, cedars, apples and myrrh as healthy sexuality described between two lovers (Song of Songs, Chapter 1). In the Bible, along with information about every other marital need, God has given us a framework for purity versus Playboy-style sexuality in this fascinating imagery. Unfortunately, as you well know, somewhere along the way to now, perfect intimacy became elusive, and its earliest echoes are from times lost in a once-perfect Eden.

So going back to the beginning as best as we can, let's look at a few things God says about sexuality and healthy touch. God gave males a seed, or sperm, to put into a woman and God created that to be a fulfilling and especial, fruitful time. It is a pleasurable time created for a couple to enjoy as well as a time to make future generations. In order however, to tend to this lush sensual garden well as married couples, let's spend some time thinking about what a precious and well-tended garden looks like.

In a garden, we see variety - it isn't always the same, right? A healthy couple isn't afraid to enjoy variety and different ways of experiencing one another sexually as they become more and more intimate and safe. Variances may be varying positions, touches, and times of day or places.

There are also different seasons in a garden, which definitely occurs in sexuality, considering some couples want more or less intimacy than others and some couples have the frustrating troubles of infertility, vaginismus, sexual dysfunction, issues from medications, more or less stimulating hormone secretion at varying times, illness, aging, childbirth, menstrual cycle, emotional issues, and fatigue to factor into their seasonal sexual garden.

With all of these specific issues, stumbling blocks, and opportunities, there are plenty of avenues for help. Just as there are a zillion differing gardening manuals, so are there plenty of Christian sexual manuals for the couple having trouble or wanting tips. My favorite website to peruse for my marital clients is www.passionatecommitment.com, a wonderful and informative sex therapy site by Christian authors and sex therapists Cliff and Joyce Penner.

Sexual preferences are not only from these seasonal issues. Personality differences weigh heavily into your sexual experiences together also. Some couples need extra space and time to process their emotions after a sexual moment together while others need more foreplay before and nothing afterwards. Others still want both, and spouses may disagree within these options too. More often than not a couple isn't perfectly balanced in their individual desires so it's important to talk about it. Don't get angry if your spouse wants to talk about sex at an agreed-upon time. Take a deep breath and leave the embarrassment to the middle-schoolers learning about it, certainly not the marital union.

TO SHARE OR NOT TO SHARE?

Spending time talking about your sexually intimate life together with your spouse is a must, not an option. For this part of the book however, feel free to skip talking to your coach or counselor, or let them know if you would like to discuss only certain aspects of this chapter with them. Most therapists have training and experience in human sexuality and do not mind talking about it with you, but you may or may not feel comfortable. Make sure both spouses are comfortable in the private counseling setting before anything in this realm is discussed. Sharing with anyone outside of this special relationship should be rarely approached unless both spouses feel the person hearing the information, for some special circumstance, won't or couldn't have any reason to use it for personal gain or temptation.

WHEN TO HAVE THE SEX TALK

Unlike the typical middle-school human sexuality talk, which is initially framed with very careful and scripted dialogue, you can and should talk openly and freely with your spouse. If you need some ideas, however, here are some grounds rules to help the conversation go more smoothly.

Find out when your spouse feels comfortable talking about sexual intimacy. Some spouses don't want to talk right before or right after sex whereas others feel that is the very best time. Some would rather talk about it on another day completely, or even while the wife is menstruating so they have something to think about for a little while, especially before trying anything different. Still others could talk about sex at any time as well as feel comfortable engaging in sex of all kinds even during the female cycle. There is no end to couple preferences in this area, but for your marital health, try to find a time when both spouses will more freely chatter.

SWEET SENSUALITY

Here are some ideas for your talk with one another and questions for one another. Take notes in the spaces provided next to each question so you can refer back to your comments.

- When can I safely tell you about my ideas for our sex life?

_____

- What are some things that have hurt your feelings in the past sexually (from me or anyone else) or have made you feel unvalued in your sexual experience?

_____

- Have we used pain to try to please one another? Though pain is titillating, is there another way of sexual relating that is gentler, non-demeaning or punitive in nature and will draw us together?

_____

- Is there anything you want to add in or try to accomplish during our time together (longer orgasm, new position, new lotion or scents, new blankets or clothing)?

_____

- Is there an alternative method we would like to try?

  _____

- What are the ways we are sexually intimate that feel best to you (position, etc)?

  _____

- What makes you feel ready to be in the mood?

  _____

- How often would you ideally like to be sexually intimate together?

  _____

- How does it relieve sexual or stressful tension for one or both of us?

  _____

- What's something we both think is preventing us from having a better sexual life together?

  _____

- Do we need to carve out room for sexual intimacy in our schedule?
- When it is okay to say no to sex? Should we refrain during menstrual cycles or certain times during pregnancy or menopause?

  _____

- If we are struggling with fertility, how can we guard our love life so we don't make sex a weapon or simply a means to an end?

  _____

- If we are struggling with sexual dysfunction, how can we address it? (Lotions, creams, pills, techniques, doctor's visits, certain ways of beginning, being kind to the other and to be patient with a spouse who has an issue)?

  _____

- Do our phones need to be turned off even for music during those times, so we don't get calls and beeps?

  _____

- What do you find most attractive about or from me during our intimate times? Are there certain phrases, comments, touches or scents that drive you wild?

  _____

- What do you think God wants for our sexual life together?

Do we honor Him and one another during this time?
- Who, if anyone, could be our accountability partners (counselor, coach, or male for the husband, female for the wife) if and when we struggle in this area?

ROCKY GROUND

Sometimes conversation about intimacy will lead to conflict, and if this happens for you, slow down and take the questions slower next time, waiting to finish the rest of this book before you talk about it again or choose to ask just one every few days to split it up into more manageable sections. Then, go back and ask the other questions at an opportune time, asking your spouse when you can talk about this. Be a good student of their preferences so they aren't taken aback by your boldness at the breakfast table!

SEXUAL ISSUES

As previously mentioned in this chapter, many married couples have dealt with areas of sexual struggle. Millions of these couples struggle with painful issues such as vaginismus, erectile dysfunction, lack of lubrication because of menopause or lack of stimulation (and lubrication varies throughout a normal female cycle anyway), illness or medication leading to sexual fatigue, disinterest and many other sexual problems that lend themselves to making intimate life less than fulfilling.

Remember not to blame or shame anyone for these troubles. That will only take you farther away from a solution. Besides, many times there is an early psychological root that wasn't directly caused by your spouse, or a purely physical cause, which is also not anyone's fault. Try to talk about these struggles openly and honestly in order to try to make some headway. If you have grown angry and blamed yourself or your partner for these areas of struggle, ask for forgiveness and forgive yourself, too. It's time for a fresh start, and hanging on to resentful baggage certainly won't help your situation, as you know from the last chapter.

Even though I encourage you to release as much of the baggage as you can safely to one another and/or a counselor or coach, release it to God first and foremost, because He can bring true healing and a miracle in this area, cleansing you from the difficult thinking around the circumstance as well as often even the difficulty itself.

Remember, since sin is also a part of the world, not all of the touches you may have received from one another or from people in the past have been welcome over the years. Many times children or even adults have been abused in the name of discipline by an unhealthy person, and some of you reading this have been either the victim or the perpetrator of such violence, or maybe even both. If so, I can't emphasize how important it is to discuss this with your spouse and a counselor you trust. Don't wait. If you are still acting on your sexual abuse, choose to turn from it. It will never lead to ultimate satisfaction.

GUILTY SEX

Although guilty sex *can* mean having sex just because your partner wants it and you don't, this isn't what I am referring to here. That kind of guilty sex or 'sex because you want to bless one another' can be great and *will* lead to blessings no doubt and sometimes great sex for both, surprisingly. Don't overthink it, just offer it to your spouse when you can. When you simply can't, don't guilt yourself.

What I *am* referring to here is that many times, some people find enjoyment in sexuality only when they have paired it with guilt, since this was one of their sexual beginnings, and unfortunately, this is true for many, many couples.

This kind of guilty sex often stems from a time in life when you experienced or witnessed inappropriate touch or viewed something inappropriate. Write down a time in your life, or a few times in your life, when you felt that you experienced or witnessed inappropriate touch. It may have been via a parent or adult figure, a child you fooled around with as a child yourself, or underage acts of sexual activity (or pornography viewing) as a teen or adult. It may even be times of self-exploration you carry guilt over or a sense of neglect you feel over not being touched enough. Refuse to carry it forward now. *God has something better for you.* Prayerfully trust Him for that and use the suggestions in the chapter to help you to move from here to there. If there is an addiction in place, seek the help of a local support group or counselor.

_____

_____

_____

_____

_____

RESENTFUL SEX

Many couples I talk to use sex as a weapon against one another. For instance, if one spouse was selfish toward the other, the other spouse will in turn withhold sex from them. Commonly, a spouse may not have pulled his or her share of chores around the house, in the others' view, so when the offended spouse is tired or cross, instead of addressing the issue, he she would regularly withholds sex. However, just as with exercise, sexual intimacy can improve function in the very basic capacities of life, so your marriage would actually benefit more by experiencing and bringing pleasure to their spouse versus withdrawing and withholding.

Don't just take it from me. God is specific here and tells us biblically not to withhold sex from one another (1st Cor 7:5). It's not for His benefit but yours. From sex comes life, both with making babies oftentimes as well as healthful life through sexual relief extended toward one another.

Unfortunately, the spouse who is trying to withhold pleasure from a seemingly undeserving spouse is actually less pleasured now too, and they lose their opportunity for the fullest release possible in the sexual realm, which typically occurs from the act of sex where both partners reach a climax. Many couples have told me that they feel closer in other ways by having regular sexual intimacy even if they feel the rest of their married life leaves much to be desired. Similarly, someone who rarely if ever reaches orgasm may still find the bonding of the sexual experience brings them very close emotionally.

My point is, by giving to one another sexually as requested within reason, you are creating more emotional health in your marriage and guarding against unhealthy temptations in both of your lives which by the way, is often a lot more tempting to a spouse who is sex-starved. The bottom line is, resentful sex hurts not just your spouse but you also, so please refrain!

SEXUAL TRAUMA

If you have been sexually traumatized, how have the unhealthy instances of touch in your life negatively impacted you to this day? Are you hesitant to be vulnerable with your spouse even though they are trustworthy? Do you carry shame or baggage forward? If you are not going through this book with a trusted counselor or coach, take time to find a mentor if you uncover sexual memories that are painful and need discussion. For more serious instances, there are counselors who specialize in working with those with PTSD (Post-Traumatic Stress Disorder). Do you need to call someone? If so, when will you do it?

_____

_____

_____

_____

Love Note: Don't try to fill in this section for your spouse unless he or she is right beside you asking you to help them in this particular way. He or she may not be either ready or willing to divulge that information at this point but they can silently make note of it without your insistence. You can never force another person to grow before they have chosen it for themselves. Instead, focus on your own memories here.

CREATING HEALTHY SEXUAL IMAGERY

In this fallen world, many people have created or been exposed to sexual imagery that is skewed and difficult to remove from their imaginations. These images of other individuals besides their spouse, foul language, violent acts, scenes from movies they have seen, or other illicit moments are not ideal imagery for the couple who wants to grow more healthily intimate with one another.

Before there was pornography or any kind of sin, male and female were called upon to be fruitful and multiply (Gen 1:28) and we can safely assume God made the those sexual parts to work just fine for this, without masochistic tricks and tools of the trade.

That being said, make a commitment to leave anything that may dishonor one another out of the bedroom, out of your thoughts and out of your entire sexual life, even if at first by putting them aside, your sexual experience is less thrilling. Trust God to lead you back to the purity of mind and heart He created you with. You have to do your part also by being patient and by willfully turning your mind to different thoughts.

The Psalmist knew God cleanses the thoughts of His children, when he cried, "Wash away all my iniquity and cleanse me from my sin." (Psalm 51:2).

Instead of carrying forward the darker imagery, visualize your spouse in the best way possible by keeping a lamp on or candlelight dimly lit so their body is right before you in beautiful lighting. Another ideal setting is to turn the lights out and picture your spouse in their most attractive postures, asking them to highlight their most enticing regions during your time together. Tell them what you like to hear from them and remember with patience that as you grow closer in other areas, you and your spouse will feel so much safer and healthier to be free in this area of life.

There are websites and addictions programs for those who need extra help in this area and struggle with an ongoing addiction to pornography or sex, such as www.xxxchurch.com.

If you do fight this addiction, you may have now realized that most likely your addiction had its root in some unhealthy past memories and circumstances. You also know freedom from it would be a brilliant aspect of your life finally under your healthy control again. Seek out help for you and your spouse as God had something better for you that won't cost you or anyone else their dignity and respect and will bring far deeper joy and intimacy!

ILLICIT TALK (AND ACTS)

Your sexual life is ultimately between yourselves and God, but most Christian therapists and coaches, including myself, recommend refraining at all times from items on this list.

- Things largely outside of one's spouse's comfort zone.
- Expressions of pain.
- Involving cruel or curse words.

- Involving lewd imagery, whether musically derogatory or visually so.
- Involving other people physically besides the two of you.

RELEASING THE UNHEALTHY SEXUAL PATTERNS

It may seem for some like letting go of this will lead to a lack of fun and mystery. Sin can be fun, remember, but ultimately brings loss and emptiness. Jesus has the power to help you to thrive again sexually, so do not fear. Just pray for God to take this from you now, before you have a sexual act again and also during the act, should the strong desires for those behaviors or images to come. Remember the important verse from earlier in this book that can offer you strength here also, "No temptation has overtaken you except what is common to mankind. And God is faithful; he will not let you be tempted beyond what you can bear. But when you are tempted, he will also provide a way out so that you can endure it." 1 Corinthians 10:13.

You can do this. Let it go, and replace the unhealthy thoughts and practices with images that arouse you that are not vile or impure but instead beautiful and about you and your spouse.

Take a moment to picture two or three of those images now of you and your spouse and write them down here.

_____

_____

_____

_____

Maybe you picture one of your first encounters, or a special venue, or a part of your spouse's body that is particularly enticing. Some couples also like to make an actual or mental list of comfortable positions they would like to try. Allow your mind to go there where it is tempted to go elsewhere during your sexual arousal phases. At first, as you let go of things, you may feel the loss strongly (not unlike the desert season you learned about in the last chapter), but as time goes on, the reward of not sinning during the sexual experience will help you to win bigger than you ever dreamed. The sex you have together will take you to new, respectful, and more peaceful heights, giving you a release that will help you to thrive in this and other areas of life as well. If you start struggling with becoming aroused, try to navigate through the wonderful FAQ's at the Christian sex therapists, Cliff and Joyce Penner couple's website mentioned earlier. (www.passionatecommitment.com)

PLANNING IT

There are many, many ways of loving one another in addition to sexual intimacy, especially for the couple that does not have sexual love in full bloom for whatever reason. Whether your sex life is amazing or completely lacking, most of the couples I work with if not more, enjoy physical touch.

Easily half of the population (aka the males) like physical touch best of all kinds of love and many female enjoy it too. Thus, the power of physical touch cannot be underestimated, because at least to some degree, a large majority of us are here in the world today because two people decided to spend some quality time embracing.

As mentioned earlier, some couples don't want or need as much sexual frequency as others. For couples like these, or extremely shy couples, it may be helpful to plan dates into their calendar to remember to have fun in this way even if when I mentioned it earlier in this chapter you were hesitant.

I have worked with many couples with lowered mutual desires that schedule intimacy once a week or once a month and because this works for them, they really make it special. Some couples have decided to offer one another intimate gestures and certain substitute pleasures when the other does not feel in the mood. Don't worry about what anyone else does, talk about *your* marriage and what would be best for you!

Although many couples feel that others have more frequent or passionate sex when they look over the hedge into another marital garden (or worse, into pornographic imagery), it is best to avoid trying to compare yourself with other couples who have a completely different set of standards since, after all, they are two different people with a very different makeup than your own dynamic! It won't help you or your family for you to think about that for any length of time.

REVIEW TOGETHER

As a couple, spend a moment discussing with one another what you each have written in this chapter. Honor as well as validate your spouse's feelings. If they have included times with you that have felt dishonoring to them, spend time asking forgiveness for those times and make a commitment to do better for the both of you and the betterment of the relationship. If you don't agree with your spouse about the way they perceived your touch efforts, relax and remember that their perspective may be different from yours and that you don't need to withdraw love and support even if you didn't intend hurt with your actions.

In our brief example of Chris and Lana earlier in this chapter, I asked you to share ideas for them to relate better in the bedroom and then shared several tangible but fairly obvious ways they could make improvements in their environment, intention and timing. After reading the rest of this chapter, you understand even further that Chris and Lana's sex life ultimately began long before they met one another.

The first introductions to sex were as children, by the very way each of their persons were respected at home and at school, in their own beliefs about their own masculinity and femininity, and in their own sexual experiences and fantasies prior to and within the marriage.

In his counseling, Chris related that he had affiliated pain with sexual experiences, having had years on the football team in high school where he was used to engaging in violent anal sex with more than willing cheerleaders and from his years of viewing abrasive pornography.

Although his tastes had settled down over the years naturally as he became a more reputable citizen and Christian husband and father, sometimes he wanted to involve various methods of subjugation with Lana and she wasn't comfortable. She had worked hard to earn self-respect and something deep within her (correctly) resonated within her spirit when Chris used rough, painful methods or spoke with curse words to her during their sexual intimacy.

She also didn't understand why some couples, especially in the media, seemed to enjoy this, and also felt guilty that she would become titillated by these mildly dangerous escapades. She brought it up to Chris and his first reaction was an angry outburst. What happened in the bedroom stayed in the bedroom and wasn't to be talked about other than during lovemaking. Lana wisely persisted in bringing it up as they talked things out with accountability from their counselor until the two of them could agree upon different boundaries in their bedroom.

Chris admitted he felt turned on when Lana showed enthusiasm for sex, moaned loudly or wore a nonverbal expressions of pleasure during intercourse. With their counselors' encouragement, they drew boundaries of safety and agreement and created a more romantic and soft setting in their bedroom. Their counselor encouraged them to talk more about their sexual turn-ons that weren't illicit, and they agreed to utilize these methods and fantasies instead.

At first, Chris resorted to the less respectful fantasy imagery to arouse himself during times in the bedroom when his wife refused to change up their methods, but when she set boundaries and refused to comply, and he agreed to regular accountability with one of his Christian guy friends they both respected. Then, she was willing to relax and let him try out more positions that were within her comfort zone.

With great pleasure, they both found that they were deeper in love than they had ever been with this added effort, mutual respect in their actions as well as thought life and communication. Lana realized she had been avoiding sex prior to this time because of this and not just the "bad timing" she had earlier blamed on many of Chris' advances.

You too can have a beautiful sexual life together. Don't wait, enjoy it while it is here to be enjoyed with the love of your life, the one whose body is also your own to enjoy!

Chapter 5

ATTACH WELL

"You're so funny. You always do what your boss says," Jasmine laughed giddily after her husband Andy told her about a frustrating situation at work. She and her husband strolled the boardwalk after a rare but wonderful date night, having dinner at their favorite restaurant.

"Not always," Andy returned, with furrowed brows.

"Yeah you do, you love to please everyone," she said with a forced smile, making sure to laugh a little after the comment so Andy knew she was definitely not trying to start a fight, especially on date night.

"Hold on, I do what I think is the right thing to do. I definitely don't fall into the category of people pleasing," Andy said firmly.

The night seemed to grow cold in that moment, the laughter of other couples around them punctuated the newly formed silence between them as they more hurriedly walked back to the car.

"Want to do anything after this?" Jasmine said as cheerfully as she could, having sensed her husband's annoyance.

"No, I'm pretty tired," Andy said. He was tired. Tired of being picked on by his wife and belittled right in the middle of a perfectly good evening. And the fact that she had found a way to bring in her common accusation of him being a "people pleaser" right into their date night was just too much to stomach.

He wouldn't say anything, but he would want, no, he would need, a drink at home. She was just too much sometimes.

Jasmine grimaced. "I hope you don't go and get blasted at home tonight again, since after all, you did promise me a date tonight and I expect that to be fulfilled. How about an ice cream?"

"No thanks," said Andy, icily. "I'd rather have a drink, or as you put it, get *blasted.*"

"Look, I don't mean *blasted* by the way, I just don't want the night to end on a bad note. And what about pleasing me instead of yourself tonight? I am not ready to go home to the kids yet."

Deflated and feeling pushed into a corner, Andy lied, "No. I had a good time tonight. I just need to get up early tomorrow and finish up some work now that I remember, so I don't want to be out too late."

Jasmine blinked back tears. "Now you tell me you're working on a Saturday? Do you have to go into the office? I don't want to hear this, Andy. After a tough week with the kids, I expected some help."

"I *am* helping you, so quit being so needy ok?" Andy said, "I'm going to work for us on a Saturday so *you* can stay home."

When the Carters got home, Andy sat in front of the TV for an hour, drinking a couple of beers and trying to forget that he had to work in the morning. He hadn't forgotten that that he had promised to romance his wife but he was definitely avoiding it.

Jasmine in turn forgot that she had a part to play in starting the argument and then spent the whole night stewing over the fact that he had forgotten his end of the bargain. Thus ended the last "date night" the Carters had for a time.

Although this scenario can happen to any couple at any time, it is a tragedy that is far too often caused by deeper attachment issues. In my earlier marriage book, *RELATE*, I talk about how it is helpful not for couples to bring stressful topics into their date nights at all, and how it is also best that they not sarcastically or otherwise poke fun at one another's weaknesses.

You also learned far better strategies for talking about conflict during the communication chapter of this book. What else, then, can be learned from Andy and Jasmine's conversation? Something even more important is bubbling beneath the surface of this hurting couple, and it is attachment issues.

In this chapter, you will learn what attachment issues, wounds or injuries (these terms are all synonymous in attachment research) are, how to recover from them and most importantly, how to avoid them altogether.

The first thing you should know about attachment issues is that almost every relationship has <u>attachment injuries, which means that one of the marital partners violated the belief of the other that they will provide comfort and caring in times of distress.</u>

Although a couple may have let go of the past hurts and wounds from before the marriage, and is trying to let go of bad habits within the marriage, sometimes they still feel wounded to the core by something their spouse did and it's not that easy to shake off, especially if their spouse continues to intentionally or unintentionally rub salt into that wound. Worse yet, sometimes neither spouse realizes that one of them had an attachment injury from even before the relationship began. In any case, knowing the label of attachment injury is less important than knowing how to get through and move on when one occurs.

In the first place, you may be wondering why you have to address attachment issues at all? Can't people just suck it up when someone offends them?

Well, while we should always try our best to be positive, the injuries or "attachment wounds" tend not to just be small offenses like forgetting to take the trash out occasionally or one partner snapping at another because they have a headache.

Attachment injuries are more severe and cause one partner to feel not only momentarily hurt, but also more significantly injured by their partner's behavior in the long term. Next are some items that may have caused one partner to inadvertently build up an attachment injury internally. If you don't know if you've had an attachment injury, it's harder to get through it so it's a good idea to look now if you are operating from within this wounded dynamic unintentionally.

Love Note: *If you have had one or some of these issues in the past, you don't need to rehash every single one or try to create waves when something has happened and has truly already healed. After all, Jesus said that we should try to forgive and to model after Him, who removes sins as far as east is from the west (Psalms 103:12). In a marriage, however, sometimes there are issues that have not been easily healed from and a wounded partner may still be reacting from a fear of ultimate* *abandonment. It is these issues that we are to bring healing towards, since one or both spouses is probably still acting out of the hurt.*

COMMON ATTACHMENT INJURIES IN MARRIAGE

- A couple loses a child or a parent and the other spouse recoils instead of supports.
- A spouse gains a lot of weight (or otherwise changes) and the other makes a snide remark or withdraws as a result.
- A spouse has an affair and the other is hesitant to trust, checks on them frequently and controls.
- A couple has a miscarriage and one spouse does not support or understand the other.
- A spouse yells at a partner in a way that reminds them of previous childhood abuse.
- A spouse withdraws from fun activities together or stops doing activities together.
- A spouse withdraws affection.
- A spouse becomes emotionally abusive.
- A spouse becomes addicted to gambling, drugs, or alcohol.
- A spouse refuses to connect sexually.
- A spouse has trouble with giving or receiving sexual pleasure and shuts down emotionally.

If you find your own struggles on this list, take heart. Most relationships involve some attachment issues, and most people can also remember a time when they have caused an attachment injury toward their own spouse also.

In Andy and Jasmine's example, Andy couldn't handle a seemingly small comment easily, and when Jasmine, in a laughing mood, joked that he was basically a people pleaser, things went south quickly. He wrapped himself up in an emotional cocoon and wanted to leave, to stop being emotionally close and to get home to a drink and his TV. He no longer felt safe attachment, although deep down he did long for a healthier and more satisfying relationship.

Andy may sound ultra-sensitive to you. However, if you knew the past with this couple, you would know that Andy's stepdad had abused him verbally as a child. He told him he always did whatever his mother told him to do and that he would never grow up to be a man's man. He yelled at Andy's mother and treated her without dignity on many occasions, and Andy, as a child, had resented this behavior but been powerless to change it, having lost his own father as a young child to cancer. Andy did in fact tend toward people-pleasing in order to avoid making waves in future relationships naturally. He did pretty well, too, earning his stepdad's respect over the years. Jasmine had not minded either, when at the beginning of their relationship Andy had also been a people pleaser toward her. As he felt safer with her, he stopped people pleasing as much and she began to feel that he didn't love her as much. In actuality, he was actually feeling very safe with her compared to anyone else he interacted with.

In the past, Jasmine had been someone he could really open up to about life. Now she too seemed to be asking more than he could deliver, basing him on work performance by teasing him during their date night of all places. She had touched on an old attachment wound that seemed to hauntingly question Andy's intrinsic worth. The question, "Am I good enough to do this job, this marriage, and this dad gig?" seemed to lie at Andy's feet and he was very uncomfortable. He felt like a phony people pleaser and he would not do this act with Jasmine at any cost. Therefore, he showed her he was not a people pleaser and would do whatever he wanted.

Without intending to, Jasmine was adding layers of untold pressure when she critiqued him. He put a wall up with her once again, and decided to prove to her and to himself, as well as that nagging inner voice, that he was good enough. He drank the nights away when the nagging didn't quit and in the daytime, he worked overtime. He managed to make his work quotas this way but definitely didn't shine, leading Jasmine to ask again, "Are you doing your best at work? Is there any way you could get a raise? Tell your boss that you need to work less or make more."

These demands drew Andy even farther away from Jasmine than he was already starting to feel since they hit that old inner nerve dead on. Her words seemed to say, "You're not good enough. You're a people pleaser and the answer to the haunting question about whether you are good enough is a resounding *no*."

Since his basic life worth had been questioned so much in the past also, Andy was unconsciously affiliating his wife with deeper issues than she meant to uncover. He lost trust in her every time she said that, feeling that she was a lot like his stepfather and not going to be stay loyal to him unless he did better and better, something he felt was an impossible request if love was withdrawn. Therefore, he worked twice as hard to please his boss so he wouldn't lose his place as worker and husband, but resented Jasmine for not making him feel safer.

In sum, Andy and Jasmine were having a nice date night. Jasmine triggered Andy's sensitive past issues with his stepfather and her when she asserted that he was a people pleaser and always had been. She knew he hated that term ever since his stepfather has used it so she also opened up, somewhat intentionally, an old would. Andy retreated, and left Jasmine to fend for her own self-care that evening. Now that you got to see Andy's wound, maybe you can more easily identify what one of your own typical attachment injuries look like. Which ones do you think your spouse may carry?

HEALING THE WOUND

As complicated as getting to the bottom of an attachment wound may seem, the good news is, healing is much easier to come by.

To heal an attachment wound, decide who will begin first and taking turns, share with one another <u>just one</u> of your own attachment issues each (something they have been continually hurt about or have layers of hurt over). You can each start with one of the less intense issues if one or both of you have several. In the case of both spouses having attachment issues (this is the most common scenario), after one person tells what they have been continually hurt by, and addresses their deepest fears from it, *(whether the listening spouse feels it was an issue or not)* the other should <u>acknowledge the courage it took to address the issue their spouse brought up and validate your deep love and commitment to them,</u> despite your feelings of whether it was a worthy matter to bring up. It mattered to your spouse and you're one with them (Mark 10:8) so it matters to you!

As the listening spouse, help your spouse to feel your authenticity as you try to apologize for any attachment wounds you have been a part of for them. As you address them, look them in the eyes even if you disagree about the matter at hand and didn't intend to hurt them, letting them know in the moment that you are sad that what you did hurt them. Say sorry clearly even if you have said it before and a few times if necessary. Let them know that you love them deeply, and want to move forward together as a team. Don't forget the important step of prayer together also. Ask God to heal the brokenness between you, the hurts of the past, the words that were said, and He will. He promises this. As Psalm 147:3 says, "He heals the brokenhearted and binds up their wounds." (*NASB*)

In Andy and Jasmine's case, after Jasmine said Andy was a people pleaser and she saw that he withdrew, instead of backing up her statement with more aggressive comments, let's pretend that she recognized the deeper injury, remembered they were on a date night, and softened.

In a hushed tone, she looked him in the eyes and said in her coy voice, "You know what? *You* are a good man and a hard worker. I know how amazing you are and I'm sorry I called you a people-pleaser," and reached across their bodies to squeeze his hand. Andy likely would have made a faster recovery, and if he was still upset, she could have told him a few things she admired about him, such as his loving character, his dedication to the family, or brought up an example of how he loved her well this week. If he is an alcoholic, he has to address this too of course, but assuming he isn't, she is on her way to helping him out quite a bit with offering love and even if he is, she is best left to leaving deeper issues out of date nights altogether.

The next day, if she had issues with him about his boss or working extra hours, she could have approached him with a request to talk about a problem during a time when he may be able to expect it. Then, she could have spoken about his work more directly but less threateningly, "I notice your boss seems to try to pull on you and make you work harder than you maybe need to. Is this how it feels sometimes?" She could give examples if he didn't track with her, while also boosting his confidence in ways that were more respectful such as, "You are a good worker and your boss isn't seeing your value. He is so lucky to have you."

Jasmine knows Andy's haunting question of self-worth since he bared his soul to her many times over the years and she could have tried to help him through that in a much more sensitive way.

We need to remember that as strong and brave as you think your spouse is, they also have very sensitive roots many times and may see even your well-meant comments as threatening to their core beliefs about themselves if they are still working on things.

If this issue of attachment injures is still a tough one to understand, here is an example of another one of their issues (a miscarriage several years ago) fleshed out with healthy healing conversation. Listen to this couple's recovery.

Andy took a deep breath and clasped his wife's arms in his, looking gently into her eyes, "Jasmine, I am sorry I wasn't there for you in the way you wanted me to be during the miscarriage. Let's pray about it together, can we?"

He continued after she quietly agreed, "I love you very much and I would like to help you to feel supported. I will always be here for you and never stop working on doing my best for our family in the future."

Andy, in this instance, didn't tell his wife that she was 'right' nor did he give a zillion reasons why he 'wasn't there' for her, things that may be subjective to each of them. His self-respect is intact.

Also, notice there is no need to mention a 'why' about him being sorry. He didn't put himself down, say that he was not emotionally present (which he had been accused of), since he isn't trying to "one-up" his spouse either. He instead took ownership for the offense (not the action, necessarily) and affirmed his deep love for her. This simple activity fulfills the attachment wound significantly in most cases. Ending in prayer is a wonderful way to seal each attachment issue, with a sincere request for God to fill in the wounds fully, in all the places and ways spouses cannot fill them for one another.

A poor way of trying to heal the very same attachment injury is seen here, "Jaz, I am sorry you didn't feel loved during the miscarriage. You must not have seen me putting in a sixty-hour workweek, nor did you respond to the fact that I was grieving also. I was not able to give to you and I won't apologize for how I behaved. However, I am sorry you felt this way."

Although this kind of apology may be a little better than nothing, it doesn't respond to the attachment injury at stake and the issue will be far more likely to resurface, unfinished, with both spouses growing wearier along the way.

This is because in order to really heal, you can't get caught up in thinking you are the one who acted perfectly in your marriage. In *most* cases both spouses feel this way about their own behavior deep down, since life is complex and humans will go to varying lengths and degrees to get needs met, and then sin often mars that so it's quite complex. In this case, Jasmine felt wounded and her feelings needed to be addressed. She didn't, in this moment, need her husband to give her all the practical reasons why he could not be there for her. She just needed to know he was still attached to her, still loved her deeply, and was in support of her as a fully loved partner. As I said previously, prayer helps to give the couple room to be human since only God can fill the gaps perfectly.

SENSITIVE ROOTS

Don't bring up attachment injures too regularly or you will exhaust your spouse. *Bring them up one at a time, and if you have layers of hurt, spread it out across weeks or months even. Your spouse should not be left feeling attacked or bombarded.* Roots are sensitive, remember? You don't schedule a root canal daily so whatever you do, remember attachment injury repair is a once-in-awhile kind of root canal thing to talk about since you are so actively working on your marriage now. However, at the beginning when people are just beginning to let their guards down so take it even slower then if needed. You may even want to confine the discussions to once-per month sessions at home or with a counselor who can help you to set boundaries on the conversation or when the two of you are in a good place emotionally.

Another idea is to mark your calendar for a monthly discussion at home about some of these deepest feelings, and to pray about it together first. If you get to that day and your spouse is already annoyed with you, try not to ask them for more just then. Wait, instead until the Holy Spirit provides an opportune time and then tell them you want to grow closer, and that you need to talk to them about something. Let them know you know they may not share the reason behind the pain but if they could just empathize and come around you in your feelings, it would mean a lot. After doing this, wait and see. Your spouse may be able to offer attachment in ways you never dreamed with this lovely structure in place, and they may truly meet needs you never thought they would or even could.

However, one of the hardest things about being vulnerable enough to ask your mate to meet an attachment need is when they miss the mark. This happens all the time, however, and knowing this will help you not to feel alone or misunderstood or ready to pack your bags. Just patiently wait and pray, asking God to fill you completely and to continue to speak to your spouse about your desires and needs, trying again as needed, and getting wise counsel together as needed.

GOD, MASTER GARDENER

If someone digs up something from your past you were really hoping not to rehash, relax. God can use everything, even the roots your husband or wife dug up without your permission, and He can bring changes in you and your spouse you never thought possible. Acknowledge to Him your fears that your spouse will never understand how they hurt you, will never ask for forgiveness, or will never change. Ask God to guide you in what you should do, how you can have hope again, and how you can find love that will nurture you through the difficult conversations.

God wants you to love yourself well too, and so during a difficult season, don't forget to exercise regularly and in pleasant ways, to reward yourself with yummy but mostly healthy foods, to enjoy a conversation with a good accountability partner, and to unload your stress to God in prayer and meditation.

Pray or meditate on the phrase, "Speak Lord for your child is listening." This is a good phrase paraphrased from 1st Samuel 3:10 to rehearse if you are trying to let God's Word or a specific path to be revealed to you. Wait and see how God brings comfort to you. Tell Him what you missed out on from childhood, your spouse, or both and ask Him to bring a unique and personal restoration, a full healing to you, even without your spouse recognizing what they did. Just because things aren't going perfectly, should you let anyone hold you back from your God-given dreams? No! Move ahead, with or without your spouse fully "getting" you. You can go a whole marriage and still find there are things they (and you for that matter) don't fully "get" about one another, and many people do this and have wonderful lives and marriages so long as they keep an optimistic attitude. People do not become fully healed creatures as they age, but if they are true Christians, they learn more about letting go, forgiving, and not staying stuck in drama. See an individual therapist or coach if you can't move forward on goals together. If you have the financial means to do both, by all means do. The Bible reminds you that with many advisors or wise counselors there is victory (Proverbs 15:22).

MUD SUCKERS

When we talk about attaching well, we have to talk about the leech-types of people who will attach to us as we try to honor God and one another in marriage. These are well-meaning (or not well-meaning) relatives, friends, coworkers, bosses, and even strangers from time to time. They are people who try to stick judgments on your marriage, and who, in their warbled efforts to make sure you are not disappointed in the future, tell you to expect nothing but misery from your spouse. They gossip about him or her, snicker, gasp and otherwise suck the life out of the marital relationship (and you!) if allowed to hang on to you. There are people who will drag your marriage down faster than the pesky mud suckers that lurk in murky water!

Who are the people in your life who easily throw out a negative comment about your spouse? Are they a parent figure, a manipulative friend or a coworker?

_____

_____

_____

_____

Be weary of people who are quick to judge your spouse, whose side they definitely don't know as well as you do. They aren't in the marriage and don't know what *you* do and say fully, so it isn't a fair analysis and *you, not they, have to live with the results.* Stay away from this kind of person. They don't have your best interest at heart and distract from your goal of both a healthy personal life and marriage.

DON'T BE A DRAMA DWELLER

After you try to work on an attachment issue, and if and when you are still feeling your needs unmet, there is one more thing to do. Avoid allowing yourself to stay down in the dumps. You can get up from your painful past, acknowledge that it hurt, and do your best to dust yourself off and move on. Remember from earlier that the Bible says to think positively too, "Whatever is true, whatever is noble, whatever is right, whatever is pure, whatever is lovely, whatever is admirable--if anything is excellent or praiseworthy-- think about such things." in Phil 4:8.

Yes, there is a time to cry and to mourn as we learn in Ecclesiastes 3:4. But in general, think on good things that are lovely and pure and don't let all of life be a grieving zone even if there are times for that.

This is a good reminder to all of us, but especially to those who dwell in drama for any length of time. It's a joy killer to you and to the confidence, joy, and goals you are trying to maintain. Unless absolutely necessary to release this to another person, try to release the leftover drama to God from the aftermath of an attachment injury, and move on quickly so you can enjoy every gift God has to offer. Ecclesiastes 11:4 says, "Whoever watches the wind will not plant; whoever looks at the clouds will not reap." Stay focused on your current goals. Don't look for trouble all over.

OUTSIDE ATTACHMENTS

From time to time, if you are married long enough, someone outside your marriage may elicit certain feelings that draw you to an attachment to them. This is more than the attraction individuals feel when they see a handsome or beautiful actor on-screen, or run into a waiter or airline flight attendant who pays them attention or tries to hold a glimpse for a moment. Those instances are to be avoided certainly but aren't cause for alarm.

The real concern is ongoing relationships that evoke strong emotions and interest in one or both of the individuals who are in communication. If this has ever happened to you, there is no shame in admitting it to God and I encourage you to do that, as well as to your spouse before it gets too sticky.

When you acknowledge it, it's important that you acknowledge which attachment injuries or needs that person is filling in you, and prayerfully set boundaries. And furthermore, if the feelings are strong, leave the situation when you can. This may sounds severe but strong sexual or emotional feelings toward others outside the marriage have no place in your life. However, if you don't look at the root cause of why you are so strongly attracted, you may find another person, at the new job or gym makes you feel the same feelings. You may find you are a walking target for being victimized by a seductress or labeled by men as a damsel in distress in need of rescue.

If this has ever happened to you, journal about why you think, deep down, you were so attracted to this person or people. Did they validate your beauty? Did they make you feel respected? Cherished? Important? Were they a good listener? Encourage you? Did they serve you? Compliment you? Fulfill a deep fantasy? Make you feel excitement?

_____

_____

_____

_____

If you still feel this way or even it is now over but you felt this in the past, tell your spouse about it, and let them know someone filled in gaps that are missing in your marriage. *However*, your spouse cannot and should not try to compete with an outside Romeo (or Juliet) who has no clue about the real world and hasn't lived with you. Telling them is instead for the purposes of give them insight into a dangerous prospect, letting them know you are or were at risk, asking them to pray and to hold you accountable, and being honest about what you liked about this other person.

Telling them they must do what this other is doing and threatening to leave or withdraw love otherwise is not biblical or appropriate. Threatening will not get you anywhere with your spouse and may have the opposite effect since they will feel your emotional withdrawal and be less likely to be vulnerable or more likely to find their own fantasy (or real) replacement spouse. It is not your spouse's fault if you have an affair, even if they don't meet all your needs. No one can meet all of your needs except God so remember the roots of your restless heart.

Again, remove yourself from the tempting situation, avoiding talking, calling, texting, emailing, or relating with this person. Tell your spouse, get accountability, learn your triggers, and ask God to fill in the gaps that your spouse will inevitably miss in trying to satisfy you. Remember, no spouse will ever satisfy another human being one hundred percent. Eve was given to Adam because he was lonely and God knew that companionship was good. However, in each of their sin, they still wanted more and brought death to humanity as a result. You have done the same in your own dark times. Humans fall short of fully protecting or cherishing one another fully, but God in His mercy, knows that and will heal, forgive, protect, and cherish you just the way you need. See Romans 8:28 for a reminder of this awesome truth!

PAST ATTACHMENTS

Although some spouses met one another and hadn't dated anyone prior to the marriage, many of you had roots planted elsewhere long before you met your current spouse and you may not have always cut ties as neatly or evenly as you are supposed to. Take this to God and if necessary, a personal counselor in order to find healing. This attachment wound can be healed for sure but it isn't your spouse's fault, nor should they be made to feel badly because you haven't given it up fully. Healing your mother, father, or ex-lover wound is *your* responsibility, especially if you want to carry forward a new legacy, so don't delay on talking it out in depth with someone you trust. Most of all, pray that God would remove these desires and give you help. Revisit our earlier chapter on letting go also, since much of this can be resolved through prayerful analysis.

Your spouse *has* however earned the right to know about the main framework of this past relationship, the good, the bad, and the ugly, so please try to honor their requests for information.

If you have married someone, however, whom you now realized may have been a rebound or to fill a missed attachment figure need, no worries. Many people are in your shoes, since no one was ever loved perfectly by an earthly parent or lover. Please, however, don't brag about how an ex-partner or parent was better, and say that you should have stayed with them. The feelings of anger between you and your current spouse will pass and the storm created inside of your partner by the spewing out of hateful words may not dissipate as fast as the words flew. If you have already done this, take steps to heal a likely attachment wound.

ROMANTIC ATTACHMENT

Although attaching thus far has been about healing wounds, it's equally as important to remember that attachment involves moving toward one another in positive ways, not just apologizing or acknowledging the broken road that has led you together. Romance still has a part to play and must be considered. Besides, it's fun!

When's the last time you were intentionally romantic with your spouse? Back when you were dating? On an anniversary? Yesterday (I hope)?

Like the Bible says, "Love covers a multitude of sins" (1st Peter 4:8), and loving gestures can and do help couples close.

Here is a list of romantic ideas to get you started. Use these or be creative and plan your own special interludes. I recommend aiming to **incorporate one or two ideas per week,** so your spouse can always have the prospect of a special something in mind from you but doesn't feel that you are smothering them.

ROMANTIC IDEAS

- Read them a poem that reminds them of you. You don't have to write it if you don't want to, just spend a minute or two Googling it and texting it or better yet, sharing it sometime when the two of you are alone.
- Grab your spouse for a slow dance in the living room, on the beach or anywhere.
- Whisper how attracted you are to them in their ear.
- Make them a card or write a special note.
- Buy a romantic nightie or special lotion for the two of you to use, especially if you're not the spouse to typically initiate in this area.
- Give flowers that are wrapped beautifully, even if a tiny bouquet, or stop to pick them beautiful flowers from the roadside.
- Write them a love letter and then mail it.
- Call in a special song on the radio and ask them to listen to that station if and when you get through.

- Write, "I love you" on the bathroom mirror with a piece of soap or if you are female, lipstick.
- Guys, kiss your lady's hand or take both of her hands in yours while you look into her eyes and kiss them.
- Make a toast to one another when you eat together, a sincere one from the heart.
- Call your spouse while playing a romantic song over the radio and say you love them and are thinking of them on their voicemail.
- Buy your spouse a romantic CD or iTunes song that makes you think of them.
- Buy one small inexpensive but thoughtful gift for them each week.
- Cut out paper hearts and neatly write out special memories that the two of you have shared on them. Place them in a special keepsake box.
- Make an intentional move to hold hands.
- Buy earrings or a meaningful piece of jewelry for them.
- Buy costume jewelry or nice cologne that is inexpensive but also attractive for them.
- Set a bath from them with their favorite items and help to dry them off.
- Sing your spouse a karaoke song or if you know how to play an instrument, practice and play a song for them. Do this at home or out and about if you aren't shy!
- Serenade them from the bottom of the house or outside their bedroom window.
- Throw pebbles (NOT rocks) at their window and let them see you standing outside with a sign saying, "I love you," or something else romantic.
- Plan a special date that they knew nothing about.
- Eat dinner by candlelight, serve a gourmet meal, or ask the kids to be your servers and to provide a romantic dinner (or if they are small, put them to bed early for a surprise at-home date with a few of your spouse's' favorite foods or games ready to enjoy).

LASTING ATTACHMENT WOUNDS

If after trying everything in this chapter out and still sensing that you or your spouse has an attachment injury that gets triggered occasionally or even frequently, spend time talking about it together and praying for God to release you both from any unwanted binding soul ties of the past, which He promises to do. Pray this cleansing verse over one another and yourself as you let go of any ties you have with sin and other lovers. "And the very God of peace sanctify you wholly; and [I pray God] your whole spirit and soul and body be preserved blameless unto the coming of our Lord Jesus Christ." (1st Thessalonians 5:23)

If you make mistakes sometimes (as we all do) from a previously surrendered attachment wound, briefly let your spouse know you are sorry you revived that wound, whether you did it intentionally or not. Remember, it costs nothing to look in their eyes (if you are face to face or as soon as you are again) and to let them know that you deeply love them and want to be by their side through thick and thin. It may sound like a complicated issue, but it often really is this simple, reassuring one another that you are deeply loved. Let them know you are sorry for the wounds they have from the past if they are aware of them. Allow yourself to empathize with them so you are less likely to hurt someone you love. Pray for strength. If the spouse seems to be exaggerating, remind this clingy spouse to get self-care, and that God, the Father who will always love them passionately, wants them to take good care of themselves.

If they overwhelm you too much in their neediness, set a loving but firm boundary and use some of the communication strategies you learned in the second chapter to make a loving but graceful exit from the conversation(s) so they can do their own work and are not permitted to zap you of all your time and strength.

I know if you follow these steps you will both be on your way to a much healthier marriage. It's amazing what a healing place a Christian marriage can be when both spouses have offered their complete commitment to their spouse and to God.

REPEATING CYCLES

As we all know, history tends to repeat itself so one important thing to remember when letting go of the past is to have a good short-term strategy for letting go of the little resentments that sometimes accumulate in the day-to-day. In these cases, as many times as is needed, come back to the steps of forgiveness in this book and commit to forgiving. However, make sure you also address with your spouse that while you aren't trying to start a fight, you are having a hard time being authentic because something they did triggered your painful memory or just simply irritated you, taking both of you back to an unhealthy way of relating. Let them know you are praying about it, and then *do pray*. Ask God if you need to confront your spouse on anything. Resolve to get better self-care this week in addition to whatever conversations you may have. Don't overdo the emotional rollercoaster of major trauma with every small nuance, just remember that keeping yourself open to God and communication with your spouse can remove barriers and keep you out of an enslaved and emotional Egypt.

Earlier in their romance when they dated, Andy had been very authentic and nurturing when he emotionally wounded Jasmine, even if he didn't believe he was wrong. He usually had no clue he had even done anything wrong until she told him that he had done this. However, since he then loved her so passionately and tenderly, he would say almost anything in his desperate attempt to win his new bride over or to bring a smile to her face.

As the years passed and weight was gained, skin began to sag, voices were grumpier, they were tired, and cheerful smiles became fewer and farther between, Andy didn't exactly feel like apologizing as much, especially when she snarled at him more frequently.

After doing the *RELEASE* attachment chapter, this couple had many opportunities to make up for lost time, thankfully.

One day, Jasmine was doing the dishes after a party. Andy was visiting with his extended family and had sat down on the couch watching TV the whole time while she had cooked, cleaned and served. Jasmine snapped at him after the party was over saying, "I can't believe you just sat there letting me do all the work."

Instead of his old persona, the one who felt he was on the stand for proving he was a competent human being and not a people pleaser to his wife, Andy acted differently. He recognized his wife had served all day, was exhausted, and had forgotten that he had both done the yard work for the party as well as shopped for the food. He wanted to relax during the visit and planned to help clean up. He said, "I'm sorry, honey. You are so special to me and I saw the way you helped everyone and made the party a success with your serving. I really appreciated it most of all since I was so stressed and really enjoyed letting down after a hard week. Would you like to relax with me?"

She was silent in the face of this new response and though she wanted his help before relaxing, she was able to soften and compromise. After he had finished unwinding he continued, "I'd like to help with something around the house now, what can I do?"

Jasmine, even amidst this gentle approach began to sob and Andy felt an attachment injury or strain had obviously occurred. Andy then leaned in with more full-fledged attachment gestures, hugging, cuddling, stroking her, whispering encouraging words to her, and simply looking into her eyes with love. (A sad lover who is used to rejection or anger during these times is unlikely to be hostile or coarse with someone when approached in these softening ways).

Since he suspected an attachment injury, he even said at that point, "Does this make you remember that I wasn't there for you the way you needed after you had the miscarriage?"

"Yes," she sobs. "I feel like I have to do it all while you get the easy part and you just let me."

I will always be here for you honey," Andy said, kindly, rubbing her arm and whispering in her ear. I just needed some time to get recharged but I can see why you remembered the difficulty when you were sad. Rest assured, we are together forever and you have every reason to put your trust in me. As you know, I don't drink anymore but that means I need to take care of myself more than ever in healthy ways and to relax on my one day a week at home for part of the day is good even if that means the clean-up has to wait."

"Okay," she sniffled. "That makes sense. I guess I was just feeling a little sorry for myself."

"Atta girl!" her husband said, "You pick a movie tonight and forget the chores. I'll help clean up after the movie. Come and sit with me for awhile." And she did.

Chapter 6

SERVE ONE ANOTHER

"Well at least tomorrow is Sunday. We'll *finally* get to sleep in before the late service," Zack said with red-rimmed eyes as he and his wife Amy were getting ready to lay down for the night.

"Yeah, about that." Amy rolled her eyes. "I actually signed up to take a meal to the Smiths beforehand, then I'm serving at church as a greeter and then there's the kids anyway. And you know Robbie is going to ask you to take down chairs afterwards. Let's hope Zack Jr. stays in bed for you too," Amy added, "You promised you would do the night shift since it's the weekend."

"Ugh. That's depressing. Did you have to remind me of that right now?" Zack groaned, stuffing his face in the pillow.

"What do you mean?" snapped Amy, "*I'm* serving the family six days a week and then I'm trying to serve my neighbors and church on the off days. That's anything but depressing, it's called love."

"Do you feel good doing it?" Zack asked, ignoring her tone, a good student of attachment and knowing his wife felt the need to do countless tasks compulsively at times since she had grown up trying to prove her worth this way. He looked deep into his wife's eyes with a sad sincerity.

She pushed down the swirling emotions inside. "Yes, I do," she said more boldly than she felt. "I get filled up by helping others."

"Ok then, there's your ten million dollar answer about whether I will get any sleep and the answer, folks, is no!" Zack groaned and gave his wife a quick kiss on the cheek. "Good night, dear. I know you need your sleep. Happy to help tonight." He pushed down the tears brimming in his already bloodshot eyes. When would he get some time off? What were they doing wrong?

"Good night love," she said in response, stroking his arm and simultaneously worrying over whether she could do it all the next day, wishing for a break and not knowing how to take it.

Service. It's wonderful, it's necessary but it can be one of the fastest ways to deplete even an otherwise healthy marriage if you aren't careful. Too many couples are happily stuck in lives busier than they can handle because of their inability to say no. Part of this is due to their misunderstanding of our Christian call to serve. As the Bible says, "Each of you should use whatever gift you have received to serve others, as faithful stewards of God's grace in its various forms." (1st Peter 4:10).

We know, then, that we are plainly called to serve using the gifts God gave us. However, most couples have not (yet) streamlined their lives into a practical way to serve in those giftings together because of the cultural (and often inner) pull on them to serve in so many different directions.

When they do learn a more harmonious serving style and schedule it in together, this part of their marriage can be one of the most satisfying, so it's actually a beautiful combination of quality time and service.

Like Amy, sometimes one spouse is so intent on serving in a particular fashion that they don't even realize serving has lost its joy for them. Many times their service has depleted them terribly. Other times, it depresses them, like in Zack's case, even as he bravely tried to stifle it.

Although service is a Christian duty and truly brings joy when done well, here are some service red flags to be aware of in your marriage:

RED FLAGS OF SERVICE

- You are at or approaching burnout.
- You don't get nearly enough sleep (consistently less than six hours a night).

- You say yes to things regularly that your spouse isn't a part of even when he or she would otherwise be with you (weekends and evenings, depending on your schedule).
- You are not having nearly enough sex (some will never feel full here but less than one time per week for many couples would fit this).
- You are not finding joy in your service.
- You aren't using your spiritual gifts in your service.
- There's no way for you to get 'relate' (or no-stress) time with your spouse because of all of your service activities.
- You are offering service outside of the home but chores and duties inside of the home are being neglected on a regular basis.
- You don't communicate regularly with your spouse and don't prioritize serving them.
- You serve on time-consuming teams and boards other than for work (mandatory ones) that your spouse isn't a part of. (Once a month men's or women's nights out or occasional groups that meet monthly or during your spouse's work hours don't count here)
- You have ignored your spouse's advice to take it easy.
- Your kids are weary of you serving because they feel neglected.
- You have a parent or sibling that you spend an excessive amount of time with or caring for when your family otherwise has to fend for themselves.

If you have seen yourself described in one or more of these service red flags, spend a moment here journaling and praying to God about it. Ask Him to convict you of any service that you need to let go of in order to meet your goals of a healthier marriage and family life.

_____

_____

_____

_____

ROOTS OF MARRIAGE

If you think back to creation, God made Eve's giftings specifically relational when He gave her to Adam as a beautiful companion. He didn't make her to have a thousand committees to serve on or desire she have the perfectly organized recipe box, a color-coordinated closet (she didn't even have clothes, come to think of it!) or the perfect yoga stance either. We have come up with these perfectionistic standards all by ourselves as women over the ages.

God also didn't make Adam to work twenty-four hours a day either, to bark out orders or to be snappy because he was tired from naming animals and working in the garden. No, He made him to do work and then rest on the final day of the week (Genesis 2:3) with the wife He had made for him. Then and only then was creation perfect.

Even though we need one another and service is definitely part of God's amazing plan, God wants you rest and to love your spouse. He wouldn't have taken the time to make a family as His first perfect human creation if there wasn't something powerfully awesome about the male and female marriage relationship dynamic. If you choose to believe this, how would or could it change your schedule around?

_____

_____

_____

_____

Now, spend a moment asking your spouse what it is *they* would change about your family schedule if they had enough time. I know that's being very vulnerable but that's a good thing in this instance. One of those most important parts about marriage is not doing anything that your spouse isn't enthusiastic about. It doesn't mean they are jumping for joy about each activity you do but it does mean that they love everything you do because they know it fills an important part of you and is healthy for your family. Stop and journal their response here and keep an open mind in the conversation. As the Bible says, "If a house is divided against itself, that house cannot stand," (Mark 3:25).

_____

_____

_____

_____

With your spouse, take a few moments to talk about the natural ministries God has given you together and cross things off the schedule that just don't fit or make sense for your family time, marital and financial budget. Write that down some of your resolutions for change here.

_____

_____

_____

_____

What things have you decided to cross off your time, marital, and financial budget? (Be specific and give time frames for each). When will this cease? What will replace it, if anything? Work from a calendar and commit to working toward getting rid of things that don't belong or cancelling them before they begin. Use real schedules, phone reminders or whatever other tools will help you to follow through before moving on.

Love Note: *If you aren't convinced yet to let go of some things and you are still discouraged about confronting your spouse, keep reading. There are many more great tips in this chapter about how to serve within your best means!*

SERVING ONE ANOTHER

Service is one of the great joys of life, as you probably know if you are in up to your ears in loving others, and the verse, "It is more blessed to give than receive" rings true, right? Being able to give is a privilege. Within marriage too, then, service should be an everyday thought, but often couples forget, thinking that since they are one flesh, they don't need to serve one another specifically. When this happens, resentment, exhaustion, or time mismanagement can make the marriage relationship very difficult and lead to depression, anxiety, temptation and sin.

Even if your spouse's schedule appears to look picture-perfect and they get plenty of self-care, it isn't the case if you aren't their biggest support. They have cheerleaders all over the community if they are nice people, and even strangers take note of good deeds in a weary world. Their number one source then needs to be you in order to keep them remembering their best sources of encouragement and fulfilled maritally. If you are resentful about serving one another, please remember that Christ came to serve, not to be served (Matthew 20:28). What can this look like for you?

_____

_____

_____

_____

Here are some ideas for serving your spouse. Go over this list together and let one another know what you would like to see more of ideally.

Ideas for Serving One Another:

Check the boxes that you would like to be served with. Don't demand, just let them know your areas of interest these days!

- Meal(s) made.
- Chores you currently do to be done for you, even if occasionally (be specific here):_____
- Going on a date out together.
- Reading a book together.
- Having more dinners together (Be specific and get it on the calendar if spouse agrees).
- Going to bed together.
- More physical intimacy or sexual touch together.
- Serving at church on the same team, same day.
- Having back massages, more hugs, non-sexual touch.
- More kind words being spoken throughout the day, like sweet text messages, emails or face-to-face.
- Having a special night at home or out weekly that is designated for the two of you and held as sacred.

Talk about this list with your spouse. Mark your calendars with some ideas, and don't be mad if your spouse has to remind themselves to serve you. Not everyone is able to multitask or naturally do these things, but what's important isn't that it's a natural process, but an intentional one. In fact, it may be even more romantic to think that someone finds you so important that they are scheduling in service to you.

> ***Love Note:*** *If you do one thing to bless your spouse and then forget because you didn't schedule it in, just pick up where you left off, check in with one another again, and get going on it. Love is never too late for a married couple.*

AT YOUR SERVICE

Serving others is important, especially if you pay attention to the actual needs your spouse is expressing versus something you simply enjoy doing or find convenient to do. It's important to take inventory together seasonally. In a garden, you don't water all the time or you'll drown out the place. As you train for a race, you vary your workout. Sometimes in marriage you simply enjoy a good rest since you've pruned, lunged, plucked, watered, planted, and God knows what else! Sometimes it looks like sitting down right in the middle of the hard work you are doing whatever it involves and simply resting as we discussed in the first chapter.

At other times, however, it looks like asking someone else for his or her perspective and that someone is your partner, your spouse. In this large garden of marriage, there are so many areas to tend to and there may be a patch of grass that has been run over and not cared for as tenderly as it needs to be lately.

While to you this area may seem insignificant and in the background, your spouse may recognize it as a poison, drying the life out of the marriage, a gaping eyesore in the garden of your life. Taking time to ask your spouse how you are doing in the service department and how they would most like to be treated here can go a long way in growing your garden well.

PAST REMINDERS

When you were growing up, how did you see your mother and father (or caregivers) serve one another? Did they take self-care shifts? Did they have a healthy tradition of putting one another first? Did one give the other weekly or monthly nights off? If not, begin fresh and if so, try to carry something healthy forward. Write that down here.

_____

_____

_____

_____

How did this help your parent(s) if they did serve one another? If they didn't, how did that make things harder? How are you serving your spouse right now? Feel free to count work outside of the home as one thing but not the only thing because that serves a wider purpose, such as providing a roof, etc.

BETTER CONDITIONS

As you consider your marriage, take time here to talk out a few things that you would like to start doing for your spouse and also things that you would like to have done for you in terms of service. Share it together and modify it accordingly. In other words, don't expect your spouse to agree to everything easily. Be open to their ideas. Here is an example.

Wife: I used to iron my husband's clothes each evening before bed but with me working full-time now also, I'd like to arrange for a dry cleaner and he does it. I would be happy to arrange pick up and drop off times. I think we have become self-sufficient and no longer ask each other for certain favors since we both know the other spouse is so busy. I would love it if he could put the kids to bed a few nights a week so I could enjoy my book or call a friend during that time.

Husband: That's fine. She could probably use more help with the cooking and cleaning also. I have been so busy I haven't thought of that in awhile. I would consider helping with the kids if we can get them to bed on time. I also like to have her help in getting to bed with me a little earlier. She doesn't have to get up as early as me and it's hard to get to bed with her turning lights on and off. A couple of nights a week would be great.

Wife: With him helping with bedtimes, I could chat on the phone while finishing my nighttime chores and then be up to bed much faster. Let's do it!

_____

_____

_____

_____

WHERE DID WE GO WRONG ANYWAY?

You may be asking yourself now, how did we get so far off track that we even fight about how to serve one another? If God made Adam and Eve so particularly for one another back in the Garden of Eden, how have many couples lost sight of that perfect togetherness and even made serving into a fight? Well, as you know there was also an evil serpent lurking in the lush and beautiful garden that God made and he convinced the humans that there was more to life than just paradise and promised lands. There was power. That enticement of something more, the lure to be better than even God, continues to lurk in the hearts of God's family members today.

People want at least *just a little more* fulfillment and often even look to service projects at church to bring that even if their conscience (or spouse) says, "Stop!" *Maybe if I go on a mission trip*, or even the innocent, *I am gifted here so I should help this person*, type of thought can feed an ego and distract you from something you are avoiding (especially something from the *Letting it Go* chapter) so be careful. Take spiritual inventory now on any possible reasons you are avoiding service to your spouse.

_____

_____

_____

_____

Have you been living under the authority of sin, giving it power to be your master? Have you been enjoying a bigger ego since others are pleased by your service, even if it isn't as healthy for your family? Take courage if so, and give it to God. Even though Satan in the

Garden of Eden was tempting, he has no real power over you unless you give it.

Instead, look to God for ultimate fulfillment, not notches on your service belt as though you were on the safety team at elementary school again. This kind of pride in adults goes before a fall (Proverbs 16:18). With this kind of thinking, you may be cheating on your taxes (or even worse, your spouse) but because you serve at the PTA and take meals to sick families, donate your time at church and don't get nearly enough rest all because you "love God" it won't curb the good guilt God has given you in regard to your sin, nor will your ministry have the same measure of blessing that it does if you are in obedience to and have a right relationship with God.

If this is you, spend some time talking to God about purifying your heart so you aren't running the guilty rat race trying to make up for your deficit. God can get you perfect freedom from even an addiction you are battling if you truly surrender it to Him. Remember this verse shared in other chapters,

"No temptation has overtaken you except what is common to mankind. And God is faithful; He will not let you be tempted beyond what you can bear. But when you are tempted, He will also provide a way out so that you can endure it." (1 Corinthians 10:13)

Spend time in prayer to God as you consider this. The world, another lover, or any amount of service projects cannot fill His spot in your life nor can any human. Carve out time to spend with Him first, and you will never regret it. As Pascal once so poetically said,

"What else does this craving, and this helplessness, proclaim but that there was once in man a true happiness, of which all that now remains is the empty print and trace? This he tries in vain to fill with everything around him, seeking in things that are not there the help he cannot find in those that are, though none can help, since this infinite abyss can be filled only with an infinite and immutable object; in other words by God himself." - Blaise Pascal, *Pensées* VII(425)

SERVING FROM A PLACE OF RESTED LOVE

If you still have room to serve out of rested love of God, family, and others, where should that lead to in your life?

From earlier in this chapter, Amy may say, "If I were serving out of rested love, it would be nice to be at more baseball games for my son. The games always coincide with my mom's insulin shots but I can't do them earlier because I work all day. I would like to make a game weekly, and also to be able to have a date night with my husband each week. We haven't done our budget just right yet to be able to make this happen consistently. Managing our budget together would help me to calm down emotionally. As for my rest, I would like to be able to work a little less so that I could get real sleep and to put my phone down in another room so that I didn't struggle with that too much. I probably wouldn't serve anymore at the church picnics monthly since I never get good fellowship in there.

Now, journal your own ideas about serving from a more rested place. Give yourself time but don't give up on finding better balance if this is one of your struggles too. Trust that God has something better for you, and commit each day and even each moment to him. Remember and process this verse as you write, "For you were called to freedom, brethren; only do not turn your freedom into an opportunity for the flesh, but through love serve one another (Galatians 5:13, *NASB*).

_____

_____

_____

_____

When you write things down and pray about them, you will probably find that in your serving capacity, you feel the need for more family and individual self-care. This is no coincidence, as we learn from Eve's early roots and the disruption Satan's temptation made. The first Christian couple had a really good balance of being stewards of the Garden and companions to one another. They had a gorgeous landscape and all their needs were met.

Don't fool yourself into thinking temptation looks for a bad situation only. Temptation from Satan looks to disrupt a good situation. In your case, getting more family and individual love may be exactly what you need, and Satan will use guilt to get you as far from those wonderful things as possible.

In our example, Amy felt guilty about not serving others (her mother, her church) but the basic needs she had as a person were not being met, nor were the needs for being a healthy spouse and parent. Because she didn't love her family well, does that mean she is condemned to hell? Of course, not but she and her family are missing out on a chance to thrive in the ways God wants for them. Does this mean her schedule needs a radical transformation? It does. And yours may also. Don't be afraid to make the changes you need to thrive. If you don't let go of the unhealthy control here, the underlying message you send God is easily seen. *I don't trust You with my story.*

Please do trust God again with your story. He never brought you to sin or tempted you and has given all of His commands for your benefit and blessings.

Even so, although God does not want you to hit burnout, He won't stop you from hitting it if you are plundering through, ignoring His instruction. He disciplines those He loves (Hebrews 12:6) and many times it comes in the way of letting the natural consequences of overdoing hit you when you need a wake-up call.

Now that you can consider all of this, remember that God has given you both a free will and every reason in the world to trust him. Won't you do that today? What could you do to make a modified service schedule built on rested love. What will you change in order to get back to this place?

_____

_____

_____

_____

In Amy's case, she journaled, *"I will start using envelopes for my food budget so I don't go out of balance here. If I could spend just thirty dollars less a week, I could pay a home health aid to give mom her shots every Monday and be at my son's baseball game for the whole game every time. I can also stop serving at the church barbecues. I will see if Zack wants to join me in being a greeter instead, so I get fellowship, or if he would like to find another ministry together. As for the PTA, I will step down from the leadership team in the hopes someone in a different position will take over and I can enjoy my family time instead during this Tuesday night commitment. I will turn my phone off each night so I can get a decent sleep and Zack and I can more readily enjoy one another."*

This is a wonderful process Amy is going through. She is starting to take ownership of her time again. She never intended for things to get out of hand, just like you don't. You may think you are protecting yourselves the more service you pile on, but in haphazardly doing this, you are actually bringing more disruption to your family. If you have children, they too need you to lead them toward service, to worship, and rest. Fleeing (not just walking) to each of these will help your lives to thrive and grow in the right areas. Doing this any other way makes you easy target practice for the enemy who sees that you have stopped trusting God enough to get proper balance. Satan uses this prideful moment of service to find ways he can make your doubt grow, your life disordered, and others resent you for improper schedule management to be sure. Service can drag a marriage apart quickly if you aren't an intentional team.

SERVICE VERSUS SERVE US

Some of you reading this actually don't serve much outside the home, nor do you serve others much inside the home. Some people are very good at self-care, so much in fact that they selfishly neglect the rest of the world. Without realizing it, everything you do each day has become about you. This is another dangerous inclination, as the Bible says, "Do nothing from rivalry or conceit, but in humility count others more significant than yourselves. Let each of you look not only to his own interests, but also to the interests of others," (Philippians 2:3-4).

It's good that you know how to take care of your own needs. God does call you to this, after all. His first command to His followers is here and the second follows, "Love the Lord your God will all your heart, and with all your soul and with all your mind, and with all your strength. The second is this, 'You shall love your neighbor as yourself.' There is no other commandment greater than these." (Mark 12:30-31). Loving yourself is noted here, and doing it well is part of God's great plan for you.

However, if your pendulum swings too far in the direction of serving yourself or just you and your spouse ("serve us" instead of a "service" attitude), think of times and ways you can service the community of God together. Are there opportunities where you and your spouse can serve monthly, a ministry at church you both love, or is there an opportunity at a local homeless shelter, soup kitchen, recycling plant, or even the possibility of fostering or adopting a child in need (this last one is a biggie so please consider this one carefully if so)?

Do you go to a particular church that needs help right before or after you are there? Do you both possess a certain athletic ability, love children, reading, or cooking?

Pray about finding something than you are both passionate about and both want to help with. Then schedule it in.

God called us to serve, to show hospitality towards others and to give to the community together as we see from Mark 12:31 and also many other verses (Hebrews 13:2, Romans 12:13). He loves to see couples using their marriages to share with others the gifts they mutually possess, like Priscilla and Aquila who were friends with Paul of the Bible and were tentmakers together and fellow laborers for Christ (Acts 18:2-3). Try to find areas to serve together that naturally use your gifts and talents and that already fit well into your life.

WHEN TO SERVE

Schedule-wise, consider what service time(s) fit naturally for you both. For some couples, having three nights to unwind during the week and then the rest to be doing activities and serving is a great balance whereas some are overwhelmed by doing more than one outside service activity per month or season. The good news here is that there is no "one size fits all" family measurement. Each couple and family is unique.

If you and your spouse are completely satisfied with a high level of service and it does not truly affect marital harmony, then go for it. Just be honest if you start to wish for less on your plate and listen to that voice if you feel God telling you to slow down or to remove something, readjust, or start serving together more. Obviously, if it isn't broken, don't try to fix it.

MISSING THE MARK

You may have noticed earlier in this chapter that Amy was a classic perfectionist. As you can imagine, she had each of the family lunches in order the night before school, day after day, year after year. Each bag was stuffed with delicious and nutritiously balanced meals and she was willing to lose sleep over any of her children on any given day if she didn't meet her own demanding expectations or theirs. Her husband, we can safely assume, carried leftovers from a similarly wonderful meal to work in his lunch pail each morning, being sent off with a sandwich and coffee for breakfast. Dinners were complex and nutritious, simmering all day long in the slow cooker while she and her family went about all their various tasks.

Before learning to serve in a more balanced way, she worked the PTA Tuesday evenings, jogged on her lunch breaks at her attorney firm where she was a successful paralegal, and made sure her husband had each of his evenings filled with family time or exercise, so that they would all stay balanced. The kids were well groomed, generally happy and smart, and work was fulfilling for a social outlet, as were her other well-planned activities. Although she managed to fit a couples' bowling night into the schedule, in addition to church each week, and to keep the house basically spotless, Amy and Zack were very stressed out in their marriage. How is this possible when everything looked so perfect?

This is because there was no margin for rest together, no time for spontaneous intimacy, which was one of her husband's priorities right now. Zack had a very stressful job and as much as he enjoyed bowling with his wife and their friends, church and the children's events, he felt strapped for time, like he was always following the clock for the next "thing," even being robbed of sleep.

Even harder on their marriage was that he was also highly structured and didn't realize that he even wanted and needed to relax more since he had low insight and his basic marital needs were generally being fulfilled. On paper (or should I say nowadays, on social media), this family looked stellar, but until he was willing to look deeper into the issue of discontentment he kept pushing down about their schedule, he was unable to see why they were struggling so much.

For a short season, he began to think obsessively about his coworker Maggie, who talked about late nights and happy hour at the local bar and grill, and about going home whenever she felt like it since her kids were older and had hobbies of their own. She was fun, spontaneous, and from the way she dressed and flirted, a very appealing woman. Although Amy was actually prettier in his mind when she relaxed at least, the tight ship she ran at home made him feel more like her son than her husband, and it was difficult to express this without leading to one of her emotional meltdowns. As he unconsciously compared her with Maggie, someone he saw everyday at work, he rarely complimented Amy, even though she was so amazing.

Amy, wonderful as she was, had a weakness too. She was exhausted and felt guilty whenever she didn't manage her family's schedule perfectly. If anyone complained that their needs weren't being met, including Zack, she would cry and talk about everything she did, since she truly was a supermom and needed a break from all of the expectations. She too struggled, not with flirtation, but with low self-esteem, since she felt inadequate and outdated as a middle-aged mom, and she could sense her husband's sexual withdrawal. Her weight suffered a major gain as she ate to soothe herself from the painfully obvious awareness that she was no longer the apple of her husband's eye. For a long while, she stuffed her emotions and more tightly clung to her children and many jobs and duties.

Was there hope for this couple? Absolutely! Since no affairs had taken place (or even if they had, there is hope in any case, obviously) and no one wanted out of the marriage, this is an excellent time to learn together. It could have, however, been disastrous had Zack not finally called for help, and Amy complied in going with him.

In counseling, this couple learned about their imbalance in service, among other things. Zack would not have minded if the house was a mess sometimes if Amy was a little more spontaneous with the evening plans or more wholeheartedly served him with intimacy versus seeming to meticulously check imaginary boxes in this and every other category of life.

Zack appreciated the order Amy brought to life, but it wasn't a top priority since he was also good at this. They had enough money, truth be told, it wouldn't have been hard for he and the kids to make their own lunches most days, and it wouldn't have hurt them to hire some extra cleaning help since they had two full-time incomes. His priorities, to be clear, were more genuine and playful sexual intimacy and more spontaneity and relaxation time at home.

Since Amy was very structured in everything she did, she also didn't make room for her husband to exercise his desires and leadership as well as he could have. Thus he didn't feel as respected or as fulfilled. In turn, her desire to please her husband had seeds of rejection from the past and deep down she felt like a failure, unworthy of love, especially since she'd been sexually abused as a child. This also lent itself to sabotaging for control in the bedroom.

The abuse had made her feel less attractive and thus afraid of being a beautiful object to men, even her dear husband who was safe.

In fact, when they did come in and learn more about this deeper *RELEASE* part of marriage, (they didn't need the *RELATE* book as much since Amy had already spent a lot of time teaching them both the basics of marital harmony), they finally began to thrive. Amy shared her history and in the course of the intensive eight-week study, realized that she had not learned to rest basically at all and learned that she was controlling because she felt a lack of strength and personal fulfillment from God. Most of all she realized that she still highly feared abandonment since she was still reliving the past daily by stuffing emotions (and food) down. She learned to find better ways to calm her nerves, replacing control, cleaning, and eating with prayer, hot tea, baths, talking with friends about the stress, and laughing more intentionally each day.

Amy also learned to focus in on times of healthy rest with Zack and she learned to trust her husband more as he began to soften towards her in his bids for sexual attention and spontaneity. Zack also became more satisfied as he gained more leadership rights and began to have a say in his own schedule as well as in how to command self-respect even if his wife tried to control him. He let her know that while he valued her opinion, there were certain things during the week that he wanted to carve out space for, and slowing the family's pace down was a high priority. When she listened, that helped a lot, and when she added sexual spontaneity, he finally felt fulfilled as a man.

Zack cared about her more genuinely again, and she felt much safer as a result. He began to pray more, and ask God for help with his interest in Maggie at work. He also told his wife that Maggie was flirting with him, which at first made Amy mad but soon helped her to realize that she may lose the man she was so blessed with, if she didn't begin to show true respect for him and love towards herself and her husband. With more access to his wife emotionally and physically, with her letting up control and with accountability from his pastor, Zack felt less enthralled with Maggie at work. He began to see her as the off-limits sexually promiscuous woman at work to set boundaries with, and realized that she was a desperate woman in need of God, versus a viable fantasy to enjoy.

WHAT'S STOPPING YOU?

Sometimes people ask if they will be tricked if they love their less-loving spouse who does not serve back, but Jesus speaks to this when He says, "Do unto others as you would have them do unto you." He *doesn't* say as they do to you, and in other passages He talks about how even evil people will scratch one another's backs (Matthew 5:46), but that a Christian goes above and beyond with the expectation of God meeting their needs, and also with the assumption that they would love themselves well through other healthy outlets. Does this mean we cast our pearls before ungrateful swine (Matthew 7:6)? No, but in marriage, many times the giving is inequitable, and your spouse is not a random person that you would stop serving when they are not giving one hundred percent back. In later years, you may well be surprised at the giving you receive. Seasons vary and life rarely goes as planned, but loving is always a good idea.

No, they are called to be loved by you and you are in a deep covenant bond with them. If they are abusing you, of course, then you need better boundaries to leave, and to get help for your marriage if they are willing to change.

In general cases however, you can still serve a spouse who does not answer the call to serve you back and many times you will both benefit because God says, "For the unbelieving husband has been sanctified through his wife, and the unbelieving wife has been sanctified through her believing husband." (1st Cor 7:14).

RELEASE TO GOD

When you feel that you are at an impasse and you can't seem to get through to your spouse about your perspective about serving, the best thing you can do is to release all of your burdens to the Lord. He is always willing to listen, and Jesus, as He walked this earth was happy to be interrupted, so never feel like you can't talk to God at any point. In fact although God tells us not to speak too frequently or to nag one another, He actually welcomes a nag session himself. He wants us to pray in private as well as commends the persistent widow for pestering the judge, who finally grants her request (Luke 18:1-8).

Similarly, He talks about a neighbor who comes along and bothers his friend who is already in bed and gets his way (Luke 11:5-13). In other words, talk to God when you are frustrated about the opportunity for repair with your mate. He is there all the time! He is eager for a chance to promise you a miracle, a surprise blessing, and a listening ear that is quick to comfort and remind you of how loved you are through His word. In Zephaniah 3:17, we hear the miraculous and beautiful sentiments of our Father toward us when he says, "I will rejoice over you with singing."

COZY CORNERS

Again, loving others requires that you take good care of yourself since you are so loved by God. Serve yourself in the ways *you* love to be loved. Give yourself healthy but delicious meals, take a weekly date night with yourself, a friend, or your spouse (or preferably all!), and overall, get emotional, physical and spiritual self-care every single day. Otherwise you give out of emptiness versus the fullness of God.

Picture a glass of water that is almost empty. This is how you are when you're not getting self-care. When you try to give, you have only a few drops to be split around to all your tasks. You are parched by day's end. No one else has gotten what they needed from you either. If however, there is a spiritual fulfillment as well as emotional and physical outlets regularly, you give from fullness. This steady stream of refreshment coming into your life allows you to give so much more than you ever dreamed to others and often you even have a reservoir of love and service to be shared with a wider range.

Remember, you are worthwhile to fill up. Find out how much sleep you personally need to thrive and do your best to come up with a better schedule to get it, decide which events or outings are fulfilling and truly family-friendly and serve there. Don't forget a cozy book to read at night or the funny movies you enjoy watching to get a laugh before bed, to ask your spouse to meet your sexual needs then if possible, etc. You are not being selfish, because Jesus said, "Love others *as you love yourself*," which assumes you *do* love yourself. Jesus knew how to take care of Himself on earth, as we know from the times He took time out to pray with the Father (Matthew 14:23), when He met with the disciples and called them his friends (John

15:15), and when He spent time with pure and sweet children whom He adored and made extra space for (Mark 10:13-16). He even took naps during stressful times, (Mark 4:38) and when God made the world, He created the Sabbath for pure and perfect rest. Jesus knows that you not being God, especially need time to yourself, so please don't just *try* to do it, *do* it. You will please God and gain so much more for the world and yourself for having done it.

KEEP IT UP

Remember to go over your weekly calendars together on Sunday evening or at another regular interval so you can plan together what to keep and what goes. If this is too close to the events of the week, consider doing this monthly and having a weekly quota of events you can't exceed no matter what. If you love a challenge, this is surely the trick. One event per child per week, for instance, or one volunteer project a month, etc. Be a good student of yourselves and keep your marriage a top priority, checking in about that so you can tell whether to add or take away at the beginning of each week or month!

This chapter unfolds with Zack and Amy's difficult night. This had occurred even after they completed the *RELEASE* program, and after considering everything they had learned and many nights of misery in between, changes finally began to unfold.

Amy listened to her gut and decided not to sleep. They were back in the cycle again, the one that had gotten them so far away from one another.

"Honey, I'm so tense," she said.

"I know," said Zack, turning to face her," You run a tight ship. You need a back massage. Come over here, babe."

"Thank you. I probably do but right now I need to talk to you. I'm...I'm taking on too many things and I need your help in getting my bearings again. I want to make our family and my self-care a priority too, and it never seems to be. I love helping people usually but I have lost my happiness, oddly. I worry a lot if I will be on time for this or that, if my dinner will turn out just right when I make food or baked goods for others, if my kids will do well on the homework I help them with, if my mom's health is failing because I don't look in on it, and more. I'm just so spent. And I'm overeating, too."

Zack related to this and said, "I know. It's a lot and I don't know how you do it all. It only makes sense that you would be fried. I feel like I am running a rat race out there too sometimes, and we just carpool and help others. But our family seems to be fragmented."

Amy said, "I've been thinking about dropping my meal delivery. I already make dinners for our family and my mom, and I serve at church on Sundays in the nursery, which I probably need to stop. I miss sitting together with you and driving together sometimes. I really need that. And I need to stop having brunch with your mother every single Sunday."

Zack let out a sigh of relief. "I think that will help a lot. I feel like I don't see you enough. Let's pray and turn the unhealthy guilt over to God. Let's start getting to bed earlier too, so we can have some fun." He playfully grabbed at her.

Amy tossed a pillow at him, "I would really love that. I need that, too, you're amazing babe. It's just that as soon as I accomplish one thing, my brain is wired to be onto the next and I think I am really am missing the part of the golden rule that says, "Do unto others as you have them do to you." If I loved others as I loved myself, it wouldn't be much."

Zack agreed. "We definitely need more balance. I just don't want you to be mad at me for suggesting you let go of things."

"I'll come to you and we can pray over any new ideas or projects or committees I want to be a part of from now on. How does that sound?" Amy asked tentatively.

Zack said, "Definitely a good idea, and if I see a red flag that you don't see?"

"Pray for me, remind me to love myself well, and one more thing, since I do have that guilt, it will truly help me when I hear I am missing meeting your needs."

Zack gulped. "I don't like to do that because I know you are serving others and I feel selfish."

"I knew it," said Amy "but it doesn't matter. You have to tell me because then I see you growing resentful over it, or having feelings for another woman. I really need you to remind me of my priorities sometimes."

"I'll try, but as a grown woman, love, I want you to try to remember this yourself. I will try to tell you though." Zack gave her a tight and lasting hug.

"Thank you," said Amy, looking into his eyes peacefully after he released her. "I feel the load lightened already. Let's check in monthly about this, so we can make sure I talk to you about this and you talk to me about it too."

Zack and Amy learned the hard way how to say no, and they had to be prepared for others' responses to this.

Zack's mother was furious when they drew back on Sunday brunch when they decided for at least a season, they would eat at a local deli after church and then go home to rest. She was reassured of their love however, when they made sure to keep up with the brunch plans monthly and also to include her in another event or two during the month. They decided to let her be annoyed so they could get the rest they needed. It was *their* family schedule, and as much as they loved her, the rat race had to stop somewhere. They invited her over if she wanted to join them at their home on for a more relaxed Sunday on the other weeks and the issue and sensitivity was dropped when she realized she was still loved and welcomed.

Amy's committees were at first also very disappointed since she actually had to drop several other things too before the weariness and guilt decreased significantly.

However, once they got their service priorities ironed out and began to give to one another in the most basic ways again consistently, Zack and Amy saw the wonderful rewards of a Sabbath rest and service aimed at using their giftings. Family priorities and successes gracefully emerged. Their marriage was now officially stronger than it had ever been.

Chapter 7

ENDURE TOGETHER

Mitch and Sarah had made it over many of the most difficult years of their marriage and were safely in the marital promised land or at least the land of happily ever after-ish. (Their marriage was beautiful but realistically still on this side of heaven.) There were tendencies and sometimes someone leaned too far one way or another toward various foibles to be sure, but as they prayerfully and intentionally continued the ministry of rooting out unhealthy parts of their marriage, they began to grow hearty and strong as a couple.

How does a couple consistently keep a marriage like this well tended? And furthermore, what if you have tried to read this book and done the *RELATE* program also, and still don't feel like you have reached this thriving point like they did?

I will address both of those questions in this chapter, as well as more important details for seeing your relationship achieve the marital promised land so you can consistently thrive during each and every season.

For now, let's look a little bit closer at Mitch and Sarah. This time, however, unlike the other chapters, I have added a bit of my own commentary and constructive criticism in parentheses on their dialogue not to imply that they need to perfectly relate and release, but so you can have just one more example of a healthy conversation. As sons and daughters of God, we are always trying to grow in love and good deeds even in our daily dialogues with our spouses.

Setting down to the family monthly calendar with a mug of coffee one Saturday morning, Sarah called Mitch over.

"Honey can we do the calendar together finally?" (*I like that she was direct, but the word "finally" did not need to be added, which implies her husband was resistant or that she felt forced to take the lead. Not necessary, since cheerfulness will make him walk over to her with more heartfelt joy versus a "have-to because mommy said so" type of feeling inside*).

"Why not?" Mitch answered with a fantasy football clipboard under his chin and a writhing eighteen-month old toddler in the other hand. (*For this mom and dad of four children, this was actually a fairly low-key moment. However, dropping the clipboard is even better, it will be waiting for him in ten minutes*).

Sarah continued, glasses bridged on her nose, eyes looking carefully at her husband, "Mitch, it's been a month and we haven't even been on a date. I don't know how this even happened." (*Did she have to begin with a negative comment the moment he came over? Would you want someone to approach you like this? Good analysis, however, on something she enjoys, time with him.*)

Mitch dropped his son gently and set the clipboard down on the couch. "I know. Well, first we had your mother in town and then the car needed four new tires so I had to work more. Then, I had my basketball tournament, and I don't think we stopped running." (*Good summary. He didn't pick up the service of negativity, but he didn't need to rehash either. Just saying, "I agree, Let's plan it." may be even better unless Sarah enjoyed hearing the fact that it wasn't intentional, which is also possible.*).

"Yeah, you're right. I was wondering why I felt burnt out. Now I know. And I'm beginning to feel like you don't care. You didn't even try to stop us." (*Blaming tone here a versus productive one on Sarah's part.*)

Mitch sighed. "I do care, Sarah. Please don't even go there. I care very much about you." Remembering his tools, he softened, "Look, I know you need time with me in order to feel secure. I know you didn't get much attention when I was working before. I love you so much, you're my queen and priceless to me. Let's do this calendar thing and look at how we can have more quality time together." (*Wow, a true moment that was simply amazing. Nice recovery!*)

"Thank you," said Sarah. "I know you love intimacy and I've been trying to keep that up too so I really need that." (*Good job, Sarah. This is his favorite way to be loved and you are right to capitalize on it and love him in this way consistently.*)

"Excuse me," said Mitch, out of earshot of their older children. "We haven't had any fun in the bedroom in forever either." (*All-or-nothing statement, a little too extreme.*)

Sarah, instead of growing defensive like she would have in the old days, relaxed and said, "Ok, let's get this calendar together and then start with a date and some fun for you later on that night." (*Good planning, guys!*)

Mitch said, "And fun for you too, girl!" He smiled mischievously. "I know you like it too, I can tell." (*Don't you love the natural connection and flirting felt in moments like these?*).

Sarah pushed him playfully on the shoulder, "Alright, you drive a hard bargain, mister," she said giggling, and scooping their three-year-old daughter into her arms to let her color in her lap. (*Understandable, but if at all possible give the kids something to do while you talk about important calendar planning or with some children's temperaments, there will simply be too many interruptions for productivity.*)

Sarah went back into planning mode, "And I want a special gift for my birthday next month too, so don't go asking your assistant to get it for me again and then putting your name on it." (*Sarah could next time could use just a little more tact, instead of labeling him as uncaring again after he made an attempt to connect. I do applaud her specific request. No beating around the bush to guess what she wanted but she needs to derive self-worth from something other than her husband too, which I sense is lacking.*)

Mitch stifled the angry feeling that came up from inside just then, since he hadn't had his assistant pick out her gift at all. He had simply talked about what he *might* get her, his assistant had later mentioned that to Sarah, and Sarah had been sensitive with this relationship. (*Mitch did good work on trying not to overanalyze this. She is simply sensitive here, like many women. Next time, Mitch would do well not to involve anyone in the planning since he knows this.*)

"Honey, I *will* get you something really special," he said, "It may not cost much money because of our budget, but it will have my love all over it." (*Nice!*).

Sarah smiled and relaxed, "Are you kidding? I don't care at all about the money spent. I am so grateful I get to be home with the kids and so thankful to just have something small from your big heart." (*She did a great job validating the work he does outside the home to allow her to stay home and for choosing to value gifts from the heart over fancy things that will fade and not hold meaning over time. Jasmine in an earlier chapter decided to work outside of the home in order to have those things, if you remember. It is a personal and family preference.*).

Mitch placed his hand over hers. "I love you sweetie, I can't believe I almost lost you last year." (*Wow, this was a courageous remark. It could stir the pot. If you do this, be ready for tears and revisits. Warning!*)

Sarah smiled, "Me too, and I'm never going back there again." (*OK, I guess he knew what he was doing. Great job to Sarah who validated the safety, trust and growth in their relationship.*)

Mitch agreed, looking at her squarely in the eyes, "I'm here for you forever, my sweet Sarah." (*Wonderful attachment statement.*)

"Ok, then, tag, you're it!" Sarah said, handing him the pencil. "You know the drill. Let's do this schedule so we can be intentional again." (*Yes!*)

Intentionality is the very word I want you to take from this dialogue and a word to be mentally taking into most future interactions together with each other. Sarah very intentionally wants to map their busy life out so they have time together, time resting, time with the kids, and time to get their work and self-care accomplished. Although spur-of-the-moment fun is also attractive and works for some circumstances, most individuals and families won't thrive as much without some planning so it's a good idea to do just what they did from time to time.

From both the words and the non-verbal dialogue they shared here, you can see that they've indeed made it to the marital promised land, a place that still has the occasional hiccup, but it is a place of maturity, of putting the other first, of assuming the best about them versus the worst, and of giving active love together. It brings much joy to a marriage and family when done well! Let's see more specifically see how this couple and others can not only reach the promised land but also stay there!

THE MARRIAGE MARATHON

How long does marriage last? Till death do you part is what God says (Romans 7:1-3). Making it through the journey of marriage is a long process then, so let's use the marathon analogy for this last leg of this program.

An athlete who rushes through the training and doesn't do proper building exercises for the race often falls down early in it.

Similarly, an unhealthy marriage doesn't turn into a picture of health overnight. In both cases, some miles or seasons come easier than others, but in marriage, just as in pacing yourself for the big event, you take it step-by-step and never give up.

Instead, as the athlete or spouse trains, they do different things each day to discipline themselves. Not only do they put good fuel in, but they also stay away from unhealthy practices.

As you continue to run the marital race with perseverance, remember that Jesus understands that it's a challenge. He encourages you with these words, "Everyone who competes in the games goes into strict training. They do it to get a crown that will not last, but we do it to get a crown that will last forever." (1 Corinthians 9:25.)

Now that you have gone through this book, what kind of training will you especially need to consistently improve and to keep up your marital fitness level?

_____

_____

_____

_____

BUILDING A SECURE FINANCIAL FORTRESS

In nature, wild forests can be just as beautiful as the most manicured botanical garden. Maritally, this can be compared with a wild, country couple with a sweet two-bedroom bungalow and nothing else to their name. As you know, this couple has every bit of a right to a beautiful marital love affair as a couple that has a mansion with three swimming pools, and may indeed have more joy together. Healthy marriages occur in all financial platitudes.

> **Love Note:** *It's not about the money. It's the people who manage it that matter to God.*

We all know stories of wealthy couples who no longer have joy in their hearts even with enough money to feed a small army. We aren't surprised, because we remember God's warning about money. "For the love of money is a root of all kinds of evil. Some people, eager for money, have wandered from the faith and pierced themselves with many griefs." (1 Timothy 6:10).

This does not mean that having a savings account or a nice home is wrong, since the Bible also says, "A good person leaves an inheritance for their children's children, but a sinner's wealth is stored up for the righteous." (Proverbs 13:22)

Whether you are rich or poor, finances often cause couples to snarl at one another, and the less frequently this happens, the better.

In my office, many a couple have told me they aren't on the same page financially which is why I believe enduring to the finish line also involves looking carefully at your financial life together.

In fact more than fifty percent of the couples I work with say financial stress is one of the biggest issues. Because of the embarrassment or tension it produces, they rarely want to talk about it with one another. This is an essential and necessary topic here and if you have stress here, it too must be brought into your work with a neutral party, such as a counselor, financial planner or life coach.

When financial stress exists, typically one person or both come from a home where spending patterns were not mature or wise. Sometimes there simply wasn't enough money to go around. The couple themselves have followed suit in their predecessors' mismanagement even when they have made enough money, and the results are sadly stressful to the extreme.

Talk for a little while with one another about your financial situations growing up. What did those early experiences teach you about life and money? If you are completing this section alone, journal out some of your thoughts here. Try to remember what your earliest significant money memory is also. Do you think that may have shaped you or made you feel a certain way about money, such as fear, discouragement, excitement, eagerness or hope?

Use the tools you learned to effectively communication in the second chapter of this book to help you navigate through your financial issues. Dave Ramsey's website, radio show or books can help greatly, Suze Orman's retirement tips are another great tool to use, and any other favorite and widely successful financial planners you know can also help.

Here are a few basic tools and tips to bring into your financial discussions even if you don't choose to address it with a financial system or planner.

1. Minimally, decide on the money priorities of the home and decide who will be the one to keep the budget. Ideally both

are a part of this, have passwords to all accounts at easy disposal, and work together to go over bills monthly together. Both should also have access to all spending in all accounts though one spouse may typically lead in budgeting and direction so spending isn't out of control.

2. Even if you are tight on the bills, make sure to allot yourselves a reasonable portion for first a tithe portion to God (many biblical scholars agree this is a ten percent portion of your income before taxes) and a small amount of "fun money" before you pay the bills. Trusting God involves giving Him your first fruits and recognizing that all blessings are from Him. He promises to bless these efforts. Fun money may be divided equally or shared on entertainment and fun or vacation planning, holiday extras, movie tickets or whatever else you think will reasonably refresh you during your savings plan during the allotted pay period.

3. Use cash as much as is reasonably possible, especially at first if you are paying down debt. It is much easier to spend excessively on a debit or credit card since the concept of where the money is going is vague. When you are slapping out tens and twenties for dinner with the family or extra gas since you ran all over town without a second thought, you will notice yourself holding onto your money a lot tighter.

4. Get one month's salary saved in a separate savings account and then pay down big debts.

5. Pay down smaller debts while saving a second month's savings.

6. Decide on a larger savings plan, such as six month's savings. Try to simultaneously build into a 401K or other investment plan even if it's only ten dollars a week. Talk about retirement practically. What are your plans? When will you make one if not yet? Put it on the calendar. This is your future. Will you be able to go on like you are forever, or will you need a different job, etc? When will you get moving in this direction?

7. Talk about your financial dreams together. Have you always wanted to own your home versus renting (a very wise investment, typically)? Do you both long for a trip to Hawaii once you are debt-free? Do you want to pay for your

children's college fund or a car for them (or better yet, pay for half of their car up to a certain limit, while they rise to meet the occasion to raise the other half)? Do you want your own car upgrade more than anything? It's fun to set long term goals together so when times are tough, you can remind one another of the prizes to come.

8. Are there other ways you can supplement income without compromising your family quality? Do this if so!

9. Plan in vacation time, even if it's staying local or going on a one-weekend a year road trip when money is tight. Look for local deals for city passes to museums, write down local restaurants throughout the year that you will visit then to build momentum, and plan well so you can do a full or mini-staycations during the tightest seasons or years. If you plan and organize, these may be even more relaxing and fulfilling than a hustling and bustling, debt-incurring trip by far!

10. Set aside money for date nights, preferably weekly, but minimally monthly. Do sitter swaps or use the childcare at your local gym for simple dates working out together. If you still can't get a date out, put the kids in their room with a movie or tire them out early so that a few times a month you can have an intentional at-home date night!

OFFER EMOTIONAL SECURITY

Financial security is important but couples are also fueled by consistent emotional security. Use regular speech and nonverbal cues to tell your spouse that you *will* endure together, like Mitch and Sarah did for one another. Though actions need to follow suit it also helps a spouse who feels misunderstood to know that you aren't going anywhere even if they are feeling like you hit a communication roadblock or your schedules are so out of whack that it feels like you are growing distant.

Be genuine, showing small cues of love each day. Don't gossip about your spouse, don't treat them as one of the children or tell others that you have to bear loving them to get sympathy or attention. As I have said several times, if someone is truly abusing you, you need to get accountability and most likely to separate in order to make real changes that will last. But if your spouse is simply annoying at times (Who isn't?), not the best communicator (Who is?) not perfectly attractive (Ditto), and you don't get jittery, new romance feelings every time you see them, then you know you are married to not an object or a paycheck or a pin-up model, but a person who is, like you, even if it is hard to swallow, made in God's image and deserving of your top respect and allegiance. You are one flesh with this person, and hurting them will only hurt you. Put away the conversations that poke fun at them, don't giggle about their many flaws or intentionally hurt their hearts in any way.

Many people have said they can't show love when they don't feel it. This is immature thinking. Love is not a feeling and showing love is not only a suggestion, but a call to all believers who are Christians when we are called even to love our enemies in Matthew 5:44. Don't you love your kids even when you don't feel they are behaving? Are they super-lovable in the teen years? If you don't have a teen yet, consider this foreshadowing carefully.

Please don't rely on your kids to support you through a fight. If you rely on your child to give you an "ego boost" so you can feel justified in your feelings with your spouse, you are treating them unfairly. This will typically not last as a buffer for your tension with your spouse, but will only increase family tension. Neither should they be in the middle of your fights or used as an enmeshed best friend. If used in this way, they will want to run, not walk out of your home the minute they can as a teen to avoid the unfair bondage of your love or to check out with drugs or alcohol. Worse, they will almost surely want to find a partner at a young age to help them carry to load of massive stress they have, and won't wait until God brings them a suitable mate at their season of maturity.

Instead the Bible calls us to love our spouses at all seasons here,

"Love is patient, love is kind *and* is not jealous; love does not brag *and* is not arrogant, does not act unbecomingly; it does not seek its own, is not provoked, does not take into account a wrong *suffered*, does not rejoice in unrighteousness, but rejoices with the truth; bears all things, believes all things, hopes all things, endures all things. Love never fails…" (1st Cor 13:4-8a), as well as here, "Let your fountain be blessed, and rejoice in the wife of your youth. As a loving hind and a graceful doe, Let her breasts satisfy you at all times; Be exhilarated always with her love…." (Proverbs 5:18-19).

Besides verbal cues, other ways to ensure you spouse recognizes your marital endurance gestures include,

- Leaving love notes in places they will see them each week.
- Saying "I love you" with a kiss before bed, sometimes allowing the kisses and touches to longer even when there isn't time or desire for more.
- Touching with a massage or back scratch.
- After a fight, choosing to remind your spouse of your love even if you are very annoyed.

GET CONTINUED ACCOUNTABILITY

I can't emphasize enough that in all of the tough seasons or legs of the journey, you need help from someone who has been there, such as an older mentor couple who is wise, a counselor, pastor or coach. As needed, these individuals can be there to guide you and have studied the terrain longer than you have and in wider variety with all of their other couples. They have simple tips for harvesting or moving things around that will keep your marital garden more fertile and lush than you ever thought possible.

Even though people won't always tell you, marriages that endure often have a wonderful accountability system in place, both in their friendships with one or two people who care about and respect their marriages, as well as in a mentor. If you've got an extremely stressful situation, tell a couple of trustworthy mentors so one person does not get overloaded by your stories of feeling defeated and in their own bewilderment, encourage you to give up or to seek out an affair. This person then, should also be a believer in Jesus and in the sanctity of marriage. In essence, hang with good people. "Do not be misled: "Bad company corrupts good character." (1 Cor 15:33).

PRIORITIZE

One godly missionary couple in their eighties told me years ago that if things weren't going right in the bedroom, a couple shouldn't be serving at church on Sunday. It may sound extreme but their point was something I thought about for years. They meant that if a couple isn't making time for marriage and yet says that they have time to serve others, they are wrong. After God, loving your spouse and children are the top priority. Our service to the world is so much more powerful if husband and wife, whom, after all represent Christ and his bride, are a team and operate as such.

What one or two things should you do to plan to reprioritize so you have more time to focus on marital healing?

_____
_____
_____
_____

KEEPING IT FRESH

Even if you aren't by any means "old" yet, your marriage will grow dry or tiresome without tending to it. Spruce things up as needed. Are you getting weary of your coed soccer league? Do you maybe want to change up your friendship circle a little and to add a couple to hang out with? Do you want to serve together in a different area of your community? Can you plan to save for a couple's event or do a new hobby together? Do you need to cast a new vision for your life or prayerfully pick up on where you left off so you feel you are headed somewhere together again? Write down your intent here.

_____
_____
_____
_____

In a garden, in order to keep things spruced up, gardeners keep winter interest plants, since they hold onto their leaves over the winter, making the garden seem "alive" even on the coldest days. A garden containing nothing but deciduous, seasonal plants just can't do that. The heartier, sturdy green winter interest fronds, in contrast, pay no attention to cold weather and short, dark days.

In a race, when someone is running a marathon, they fuel up and continue to hydrate and eat small snacks so they won't starve themselves for the journey.

In order to go the distance maritally you need proper rest, you need to embrace via physical touch, you need to let go of any baggage of the past that is literally weighing your relationship down in bitterness and unforgiveness, you need to attach well to your spouse and to be loyal to one another. You also need to serve one another, which involves helping one another out in your areas of weakness. These things will all help you to endure to the end.

Finally, if you are weary from the long journey and just need to let your stress go, remember that Jesus called you to give Him your every burden. Marriage really can be a tough journey, just like a marathon, just like tending a garden, but even more difficult because it is an entire life commitment and it's a combination of two people who are imperfect. When it seems too difficult to bear, when it's been a long time since you've had any "marital promised land moments" or if you wonder if you will ever arrive, remember this wonderful passage.

"Come to Me, all who are weary and heavy-laden, and I will give you rest. Take My yoke upon you and learn from Me, for I am gentle and humble in heart, and you will find rest for your souls." (Matthew 11:28-30).

Jesus promises that He is the great romancer of your heart, and if you will give Him your every burden you will be satisfied with exactly what you have, even if it isn't how you envisioned life would be. Remember not to make your spouse or your children idols on the journey, but work toward embracing God's wonderful gifts in mature fortitude (courage during the painful journal). Thank Him each day for His promises in His word, His gifts in your family blessings and His gifts in your health and personal giftings. You can choose each day to live well despite your spouse's choices, and the tools in this chapter can help you to stay steady during the hardest legs of the journey!

ADVENTURES TOGETHER

Don't forget to allow adventures to be part of your life together also. With children, mortgages, older age, and schedules can come stagnation and boredom maritally, especially without intention to keep adventures along the way. This can occur even with regular date nights and scheduled-in times of romance. Sometimes people are tempted to have affairs because the new person they have their sights on (basically an exciting object to them at this point) brings a rush and sense of adventure they just can't manufacture from the typical family schedule packed with scouts and soccer and also many times, a lack of excitement.

Lack of adventure certainly *does not* give anyone the right to look elsewhere to another spouse. Jesus tells us that we commit adultery if we entertain these kinds of scenarios even in our heads (Matthew 5:28). (And He will also provide plenty of adventures for you!)

Still, when looking at how you can enjoy one another for the long haul, keeping a sense of adventure in your life together is key. The early Christian church didn't *need* to schedule these in. The church at that time had to be on the move or they would be killed! Jesus escaped near-death situations plenty of times in his ministry and He and His disciples had their share of wild boat rides as you know.

The apostle Paul met a Christian couple, Priscilla and Aquila just after they as Christian Jews had been thrown out of Rome by Claudius (Acts 18:1-3) and they had to set up camp (literally, as tentmakers) in a new country. Living in the great wide outdoors as they often surely did, moving cross-country, and their very lives being regularly threatened provided all the adventures they needed.

Today's Christian church in America isn't as extreme, thank God but to avoid stagnation, try out some new ideas. There are opportunities for Christian-specific adventures, such as worldwide missions trips, which are a wonderful way to fulfill the Great Commission (Matthew 28:19-20) as well as to have an adventure. But this is not the only way and sometimes you don't need more ways to serve as you learned from Amy and Zack.

Sometimes you need some adventure that is simply time together as a couple. Dreaming about this and especially planning for it can give your marriage just the thrilling boost it needs! Use the following space to journal what some of your favorite potential adventures could be together. You can also list things you did together in the past that you would like to repeat. Some couples enjoy planning a skiing adventure, an adult day (no kids) at the roller coaster theme park, another wants to a hike a trail together, another isn't into physical challenges so would like to learn a language together and then travel to Mexico, Canada or even Europe to try it together. Other couples may want to climb a mountain peak or skydive or to start a challenging gourmet cooking class together in their own home every Tuesday night.

The laughter and fun, hard work and challenge that will come from any one of these adventures will find you with more fun and joy in your marriage, so take some time to dream big together. Start saving a jar of money or a separate banking account for these adventures. This won't happen without lots of planning and hard work but the adventures together can be thrilling and will surely give both of you more gusto (and stories!) for the long haul.

CHOOSE YOUR OWN ADVENTURES

Some couples will want more low-key adventures and that is okay, while some want wilder ones. It is up to you as a couple, and not every adventure has to be together if one dreams of skydiving and the other resists, etc. Whatever the wonderful adventure, try to be there for your spouse in their personal dreams and to cheer them on as they take on smaller adventures individually. List here the adventures you may want to do on your own with your spouse's support. If they don't agree now, don't rush it and take time to enjoy the thought of it. Pray together and write down your thoughts about these potential adventures also!

Chapter 8

TIME TO RELEASE

Todd and Elizabeth came to see me for a marital tune-up. They were committed to one another but often had extreme outbursts where one of them felt the marriage, after twenty years, was hopeless. On the surface things seemed okay; he was a successful computer programming engineer and a good dad after the workweek, too. She was a part-time preschool administrator who loved her job. Still, even with good jobs and a pleasant family, they kept running into roadblocks and needed to have a safe place to vent and to reconnect. After they had completed the *RELEASE* program, which took them about two and a half months, ending the journey of professional marital accountability for this volatile couple was not an option. Unlike some couples who learned the tools and had entered the marital promised land (or at least the land of happily ever after-ish) like champs, this couple knew they needed continued counseling in order to both survive and thrive.

The good news however, was that since they had already gone through so many cycles of learning together, when new offenses were made, the reconnection time was much more easily attained during and increasingly between the counseling visits. After six months of checking in regularly on a monthly basis, they decided to call only as needed. They came in for a tune up about once a year after that when big things happened, such as a new baby during one season, and at a later date when Elizabeth lost her job.

They continue to email me to this day and I am happy that not only are they maritally peaceful but that they are serving God, family, and others quite well!

Remember, if you are like Todd and Elizabeth and tend to have marital dramas and need tune-ups or regular work to keep it strong, that's okay. Just because your marriage takes works doesn't make it any less beautiful or meaningful. Think of the Sphinx, a botanical garden you've visited, the Sistine Chapel, or any other breathtaking and mesmerizing art piece. *Many* things that are beautiful take a tremendous amount of work but the results can be astounding.

If you continue to work at it, how many people will be influenced positively by your marriage either directly or indirectly? It's fun to realize that there is no end to the pay-it-forward kinds of love that will carry on for generations with your sure and steady commitment to love God, spouse, neighbor, and self well along the way.

You too now have all the training tools you need to rest well, to communicate effectively, to let go of the unhealthy fears you carried forward from your past, to embrace sexual intimacy more, to attach well to your spouse, to serve others, and to endure to the finish line! One more thing is central to remembering throughout the journey. Although I don't know everything about you or your marriage, and may not have covered every single one of the issues you've had, I do know one thing about you. I know you need God for the journey.

Love Note: Without God's help, true marital thriving is impossible.

When you stay close to Jesus, you remember that He gives you everything you need to carry out the covenant to love your spouse through both the good times and the bad. Instead of pointing fingers each day, ask yourself, "Am I relating and releasing to the best of my ability?" If not, pop open your toolboxes (the *RELATE* book and this book as well) for some *R & R* review.

More importantly, pop open the Bible. You will learn wonderful things about moving forward. Remember, "You can do all things through Him who gives you strength! (Phil 4:13). Thank you for being part of this journey of growth. Your marriage will truly make this world a better place! Send me your testimonies and questions or to get started coaching with me, write me @ Christa@ReflectionsCC.com.

ABOUT ME

In addition to authoring *RELEASE and RELATE*, I have written a devotional book for moms (*Messy Buns and Cartwheels, A 52-Week Devotional for Busy Mothers*). I also blog (christahardin.com) and write monthly devotionals for www.thelife.com. I work both locally and globally as a relationship coach and own a practice called Reflections Counseling Center in southwest Florida. I love date nights with my hubby, hanging out with my kids and the kids at church, teaching, playing tennis, jogging, sunshine, hiking trails and spending time in big cities when I can.

I earned a Master of Arts degree specializing in Clinical Psychology with a special emphasis in marriage from Wheaton College of Illinois (as well as a Bachelor of Arts in both communication and psychology from Eastern Michigan University). In my work, I focus on marriage, women's issues and family coaching.

SPECIAL THANKS

I would be remiss if I didn't thank the wonderful couples I have worked with in Illinois, Michigan and Florida thus far. I have learned something important about human kindness and love from every single one of them. I'm so honored that these brave individuals have vulnerably opened their hearts to me in the hopes for growth. I will continue to seek wisdom for our work together and to share what I have learned over the years.

The teachers, supervisors, and co-therapists and coaches I have known in my psychology and communication training have taught me so much about life and counseling also. I am thankful for their amazing knowledge, training and encouragement I have learned from them in various office settings, as well as at good old Wheaton and EMU!

My family and friends have also given me countless great tools along the way also and have been fantastic editors of many of my works. An especial thank you to Lely who reminded me of the beauty of adventure in marriage, and to Abbie, Stacey and Katie for being my closest friends for pretty much the entire course of married life. To Holly and William, thank you for being a special couple friend to us here in Florida, it's been such a breath of fresh air to have friends that spur us on toward love, good deeds, and loads of fun! I am so very blessed to have every one you reading this book, too. God's blessings upon you!